I0145724

THE LAWS OF
TRUTH

THE LAWS OF
TRUTH

*Harnessing the force
that guides our lives*

KEVIN MICHAEL BEALL

NEW BRIDGE PRESS
DENVER, COLORADO

NEW BRIDGE PRESS
P.O. Box 6346
Denver, CO 80206

Copyright © 2008 by Kevin Michael Beall

All rights reserved. This book may not be reproduced in whole or in part, or transmitted in any form, without written permission from the publisher, except by a reviewer who may quote brief passages in a review; nor may any part of this book be reproduced, stored in a retrieval system, or transmitted in any form or by any means electronic, mechanical, photocopying, recording, or other, without written permission from the publisher.

Publisher's Cataloging-In-Publication Data
(Prepared by The Donohue Group, Inc.)

Beall, Kevin Michael.
The laws of truth : harnessing the force that guides our lives / by Kevin Michael Beall.

p. ; cm.

Includes index.
ISBN: 978-0-9825141-0-8 (hardcover)
ISBN: 978-0-9825141-1-5 (pbk.)

1. Truthfulness and falsehood—social aspects. 2. Self-actualization (Psychology). 2. Conduct of life. 3. Vital force. I. Title. II. Title: Truth.

BF637.T77 .B43 2009
121
ISBN 978-0-9825141-1-5
10 9 8 7 6 5 4 3 2 1

ACKNOWLEDGMENTS

I am deeply grateful to Lori Creevay for the many years of support and guidance. I am indebted to Richard Lyke, Ph.D., for his review, suggestions and input. My heartfelt thanks go to Annie Berardini and J.B. Doze for their expertise in editing the manuscript. Also, I offer my appreciation to Michael McCarthy for his creative and artistic contribution and introducing me to Ron Kelley, whose skilled photography captured the picture for the cover. My thanks go to John Balkwill, of Lumino Press, Santa Barbara, California for his assistance and skill in transforming the manuscript into a book.

I would like to thank the people who have shared their journey with Mary and me in their desire to find healing and growth in their lives. Their strength and courage has touched me deeply and has profoundly shaped my understanding the Universe.

Finally, truly the greatest gift in my life of which I offer my deepest gratitude, is to Mary, my wife, whose love, encouragement, and vision inspired and fostered the writing of this book.

CONTENTS

INTRODUCTION

THERE ARE FUNDAMENTAL Truths of the Universe and drawn from these are *The Laws of Truth*. These laws describe the forces that create and determine the very basis of our experience of reality. There are many forces in the Universe; some have effects on us that are quite physical like gravity, inertia and momentum, but there are also "energetic" forces that affect us in other ways. These energetic forces influence our experience of life in areas such as health, relationship, prosperity, abundance, and personal growth. They affect us regardless of our awareness and knowledge of them or our belief in them. We do not think much about the law of gravity, but it has a profound and constant influence on us. The forces that *The Laws of Truth* describe are no different; they have tremendous impact on us and yet many of us are unaware of what they are and how they work.

Truth is a tremendous force in the Universe and in our lives. It shapes our experiences and directs our expressions. It can inspire us and it can bring us to our knees. Our Truth is our reality. It is what we believe about ourselves and the world we live in. What we believe makes each one of us unique. Everyone's Truth is different, however. Truth is both universal and individual. This is perplexing. Is there just one Truth or are there many? We definitely see a world full of people with many different versions of it. Are some Truths better than others are and are some Truths really false? Truth has so much power and influence in our lives it makes sense to understand it as fully as we can. We can then use that understanding to help us create the experience of life that we desire.

Truth is a real force; it is much more than concept or philosophy. As we will see, its remarkable power shapes our very reality. Truth and reality are closely bound together, and understanding their relationship can change our life. There is a very real structure to Truth and it is built from real energetic forces that hold it together and make it function in each of our lives in a certain way. From that structure, function and relationship, we can draw up laws that describe and explain how it works. That is what this book is about: *The Laws of Truth.*

The Laws of Truth are like tools. When they are used with knowledge and skill, they can produce remarkable results. With conscious awareness, we have the ability to use these powerful laws with focus and intention. This enables us to change and direct our life in ways that are very positive and expansive. Because these Laws are so fundamental and universal, they can be used to facilitate, develop and enrich many areas of our lives: personal growth, relationships, business and government. Not only do these laws help us understand and explain many aspects of our life experience, but they also reveal to us the remarkable power and position that we have in the Universe–individually and collectively.

The Universe is everything that exists.

Throughout this book, I refer to the Universe. We all have an idea of what that is and what it means to us. Part of my purpose is to reinforce, challenge and expand our understanding of it.

The Universe is everything that exists. Beyond physical matter, the Universe is also made up of dynamic energetic forces that move, flow and interact on a scale from the most infinitely small to the most infinitely grand. It is unified, marvelous and magnificent.

The Universe, in form, is ever changing, expanding out into infinity, creating for us the very fabric of time and space in which we exist. I feel we are called to expand with it, to go beyond the seeming limits of our physicality to realize the fullness of what we truly are. Contained within the Universe is all that was, all that is, and all that will be. We are subject to its forces and, at the same time, set free by its infinite potential and possibilities.

We can learn to use the forces of the Universe.

If life were a game, then part of the game would be learning the rules and then being able to apply them successfully to reach our goals. In life, we learn the rules as we play along. The "rule book" of life that we create for ourselves, though, can have inaccuracies and misleading information. It also can be incomplete and not prepare us for the many challenges that we face and choices that we have to make in life. The Laws of Truth is not a "rule book" for life, but rather a "guide book." We are not required to play by it–it is a matter of choice–but when we know the rules, we can play the "game" more successfully.

We know, however, that life is not a game. It is quite real and how we live it requires our conscious attention. Who we are and how we act in life has consequences. These consequences can be far reaching, way beyond what we may have ever considered. That is because the forces that are within the Universe, which we have at our disposal, have tremendous power–the power to do positive or negative. We are often engaging those forces without our awareness and comprehension of their strength, direction, and scope. Without conscious understanding of our power, we are like children playing with guns or teenagers conceiving a child. Understanding these forces is vital. We need to know the potential of the forces that we hold in our hands and our responsibility for the creative power we carry within us.

When we have knowledge, we have power. Knowledge gives us the ability to make informed choices. If we are unaware of the possibilities that are available to us, then we are limited and have few options in life. When we have awareness and knowledge, we have the ability to choose the best paths towards the goals that we desire for ourselves and for our world. Success in life can come to us when we are able to use our power in a wise and productive way towards reaching our goals.

There are differences between The Laws of Truth and the laws of man. The Laws of Truth describe forces that transcend man's laws. Man's laws are not always in alignment with the Universe. Because we have free will, we have the ability to act with or against the natural forces within the Universe. Often, man's laws go against these natural forces. When man's laws are not in alignment with the Universe, much strife, struggle and conflict can result. The laws of man often create barriers to growth and limit the full potential that exists within us.

From the very early civilizations of humankind, there has been an effort to create a system of laws that work well. Some systems have worked better than others in their ability to meet the needs of the people, individually and collectively. Often, power is shifted towards a few and individual power is thwarted. These types of systems often end up being structured to maintain the needs of those in power, rather than those of the individual. They can require considerable effort to keep them in place because they are not in alignment with The Laws of Truth. To maintain them, forces in the forms of military, political or economic powers are required. When such external forms of power are necessary to maintain a system, this can be an indication that the system is out of alignment with the natural forces of the Universe. Man's laws are often created from fear, a perceived threat, sometimes real and sometimes not. Often the purpose is to control, dominate and subjugate, rather than support, encourage and liberate.

To create structure, exercise control, and protect rights, there are costs that must be weighed. Man's laws often struggle with this issue. It is always about finding the balance between that which is best for the individual and that, which is best for the "collective," to maximize individual rights and freedoms and, at the same time, still have some consensus and shared goals that bind the group together.

Many governmental structures have struggled because the emphasis often ends up shifting too much towards the goals of the group at the expense of individual freedoms. Some governmental structures have thrived because of their ability to support individual rights and freedoms. The strength of any system is the result of the strength present in its parts. Systems that build on the strength of individuals and their unique potential, and allows them the freedom to express that potential would have the most promise of growth and development.

Within man's systems there are varying influences: political, economic, and social etc. As a result, man's laws often change to fit the circumstances of the time. The Laws of Truth are different, for they describe forces that exist, have existed and will always exist in the future, independent of man's creations. For example, man can decide to build a dam to control the natural flow of a river. At first, the dam will stop the flow of water for a time, but the water will keep coming and in time will fill the dam. The decision will have to be made to open the valve and let the water flow out of the dam or it will overflow and continue on its course. The forces of the Universe do not go away. They may ebb and flow here and there, but they are ever-present and ongoing. Humankind may make use of these forces by diverting, directing and channeling them to meet our needs. However, The Laws of Truth describes forces that are outside of man's ability to create or eliminate. They are ever-present and on-going. This is why understanding these forces is so important. The Laws of Truth need to be a consideration in any endeavor that we choose to engage in, whether it be our own personal lives, a business, or even a system of government. If we ignore these forces and their relationships, then we are going about life haphazardly. When we disregard The Laws of Truth, we are weakening our ability to live in a productive, harmonious and lasting way with each other and with the Universe. When we engage them consciously, actively, with intention, we flow with the Universe and it flows with us.

Life can be easier if we learn to be and act in alignment with The

Laws of Truth. Much of our struggle as human beings comes from our lack of conscious awareness of how the Universe really works. We are often fighting against the current, against the natural flow of the Universe. Many of our struggles can be transformed or even eliminated. We have the choice to live life much differently. Learning to use the powerful forces of the Universe can facilitate our lives. We can try to move a large rock with our bare hands and fail or we can exert the same force using a lever and succeed. Success can simply be a matter of understanding and then using The Laws of Truth.

We are a part of the Universe.

This book is not only about the Universe, but is also about us. We are a part of the Universe and it is a part of us. These laws not only describe the powerful forces out there, they also describe the powerful forces that are within us. The two can not be separated. To understand one is to understand the other. One purpose of this book is to help us build the understanding that the Universe and we are not separate things, but intrinsically interconnected. It is like a scientist trying to understand a tiger by studying it in a cage within a laboratory. The scientist would only learn a part of the picture. The tiger is more than just a biological mass of cells. The fullness of the tiger can only be understood in its habitat, where and how it lives its life in nature. The environment in which it lives is as much a part of the total picture as is the tiger itself. The two interact with each other to create a masterpiece of creation. The full picture of the tiger cannot be understood without the environment, nor can the environment be understood without the tiger; the two must be understood together.

We are no different. In order to understand ourselves, we must learn about the Universe that we live in, what it is and how we exist in it. We must understand how we interact with it and how it interacts with us. If we separate ourselves from the Universe, we cannot understand the Truth of who we are, nor can we understand the Truth of the Universe. One of humankind's greatest misunderstandings (and the one that gets us into the most trouble) is that we believe and act as if we are separate from the Universe.

We can venture forth into a greater understanding.

Humankind can learn and gain knowledge in many ways. However, there has been a growing bias or shift in what we "value" and believe is real. From all the technological success that has come through science, science has taken a more and more prominent role in determining how we see reality. Within science there has developed an orientation called "scientific skepticism" that has also spilled over into our modern day culture. This mindset is one in which all is doubted that cannot be validated through scientific methods. By its very nature this frame of reference can limit, and I believe has limited, our ability to expand our knowledge of reality. There is no doubt that the scientific process of experimentation has been a valuable tool in learning about the Universe. However, major strides have been made in other ways. Many times our knowledge leaps forward not through the deliberate step–by–step process of experimentation and data collection, but by luck, "accidents," and pure genius. Often scientists are guided not by theory, reason or logic but by a "gut" feeling or intuition. Are these "illogical" methods or phenomenon invalid if they result in real knowledge?

Can science measure the un-measurable? For now, the answer is no. Science is presently limited to the tools it has in its toolbox. Beyond our capacity for measurement, we must then infer, theorize and postulate. There are areas where we have struggled to measure and quantify and have had to settle for less. Is an electron here or there? We cannot say exactly and so we must settle on a prediction. How small is the smallest sub-atomic particle and just how large is the Universe? When we reach the limits of what we know to be the Universe, does it end there? Is there a sign that says, "Dead end, turn back?" Some people seem to see such a sign and believe that is all that there is and they often do turn back. Some, though, see that only the map ends, not the Universe, and are willing to venture forth. To say that reality is just what we know, is science at its worst and narrow-mindedness at its best. We must understand the strengths and limitations of science and not overburden it beyond its capacity. Science is not our only way to understanding. Knowledge can come to us in many ways, not just one way. When we limit Truth to one channel, we limit our resources and avenues through which knowledge and understanding can flow.

We have bound ourselves and limited our potential by accepting a very limited view of the world, much like the time when we thought the world was flat and that sailing far from home was foolish. I am asking us to set sail and to chart a new course in our lives—beyond the harbors of convention. It is time to step forward into a new understanding of ourselves and of the Universe we live in—into a new understanding of our Truth.

As we will see in Chapter 1, there is an interconnection between everything. The Laws of Truth are no exception. They are all interconnected and work in relationship to each other. As we become more conscious of The Laws of Truth and begin using them with intention, we will see how they each support and interact with each other.

The Laws of
TRUTH

I.

THE FIRST LAW OF TRUTH

THERE IS AN INTERCONNECTION
BETWEEN EVERYTHING

EVERYTHING IN THE UNIVERSE is interconnected to everything else. We are connected to everything and everything is connected to us. What we do affects everything else, and what others do and what goes on in the Universe affects us. We are not isolated beings living in a world of isolated beings, things and events. Each and every person, thing, and event plays a role and serves a purpose.

The interconnection of the Universe
is not always apparent.

Often, on the surface, there appears to be no apparent connection between people, things, and events. Sometimes it even looks like chaos. However, even chaos is beginning to be understood by scientists, and theories are being developed to explain and understand it. There was a time when we saw events such as severe weather phenomenon and earthquakes as freak acts of nature, but as we have gained understanding of the patterns and relationships that exist, we have become knowledgeable of why such things occur. Just like the ocean, looking at the surface gives little indication of what lies below. The Universe is infinite, diverse and complex, and yet there is a system of relationships and very real interconnections between each and every element and each and every event.

One way to visualize this interconnectedness of everything is to imagine a pond of water. Imagine a drop of rain falling from the sky and hitting the surface of the pond. The impact of the raindrop sends out a ripple that moves out from the point of impact in ever increasing concentric waves. This takes place because of the fact that all of the molecules of the water are connected to each other. When one molecule of water is moved in a particular direction it must push on the molecules in front of it, and those behind it flow into the space made by the molecules moving away. There is an energetic pulse that travels through the pond. This is the so-called "ripple effect" and is a physical example of how interconnected elements interact with each other. The Universe is like an immense pond of water, each and every part interconnected to every other part. Because of this connection, each part has the ability to affect and be affected by the whole.

The Universe is interconnected in many ways.

Everything within the Universe is interconnected, not just in one way but also in many ways and on many different levels. There is a network of interconnection.

There is ecological interconnection.

Ecology is the science of the interrelationship of organisms and their environment. The ecosystem, which is the environment and the organisms that live in it, is a wonderful example of interconnection. No living organism can exist on its own. All life forms require the support of many other things. For example, some very basic needs of a tree are soil, water and sunlight. With these elements, a tree is able to grow and mature. Eventually, over time, the tree is able to provide food and shelter for many other forms of life. The birds are drawn to trees because they provide fruit, nuts, or a place to build a nest. The birds in turn eat the fruit of the tree and help to deposit the seeds of the tree over a wider range, helping the tree to establish more of its kind, which in turn provides even more food and shelter and so on. As the number of trees increase, there becomes a small forest of trees. Over time the forest develops, increasing the supply of food and shelter and allowing the support of animals higher up on the food chain like owls and foxes. The birds, mice and other prey that are dwelling in the forest then provide food for these predators. The forest is able to establish and maintain itself because of a system of interrelationships between all the forms of life that co-exist within it.

Earth, and all of its living forms, is a very complex system of interrelationships. These relationships are sometimes quite apparent, other times quite elusive. We have begun to understand the balance of life, the beautiful way in which nature is able to support all the life forms. Each living thing plays a role and fills a niche. In this immensely diverse ecological system, we are beginning to see that an impact in one area can affect a chain of events (like a row of dominos) that can have dramatic results in other areas. We have seen areas of our planet greatly affected by the loss of seemingly insignificant organisms. In addition, we are coming to the realization that every part is important, that the mere existence of something means that it is serving the whole in some way. We are important parts and so is every plant and animal with which we share the planet. In addition, the things that support the basis of life, sunlight, air, water and minerals, are also just as important. We need all of it.

There is social interconnection.

We are not only organisms in an environment; we are also beings of relationships built on our social connections to each other. These social relationships are the basis of our civilizations. We all have a social identity with each other. There is the basic family unit that we form. This basic relationship is a foundational component of civilization. Each person plays a role in the family unit that in some way supports and/or benefits from the relationship. As social beings, we have advanced our civilizations, to a large degree, by our ability to form strong social interconnections with each other. We exist in a network of these social relationships. These relationships take many forms outside of the family unit. We have a network of people with whom we interact. There are friendships, school, work, church, club relationships and many more. All of these relationships form a network that helps us to support and enrich our lives, as well as contribute to the lives of others. Some of us develop quite extensive networks and others have limited ones. We often see people get into trouble and fall through the cracks of society because their connection to the social network has been broken. The larger and stronger our network is, the easier our life becomes because of the resources that are available to us. These relationships work and thrive when we support each other in meeting the goals that we have as individuals and as a group. These social relationships are built on shared beliefs, shared purposes and shared actions.

There is economic interconnection.

We also live within an economic system built on monetary relationships. There is a network of channels in which our money flows. We earn it, we spend it, and sometimes, when we are able, we save it. The money that we earn goes to pay for our individual expenses and, in the form of taxes, goes to support public services that benefit the whole and the individual. Our economic system is built on individuals acting in a way that supports the system. There are local, state, national and international economies all interacting with each other. Money is constantly flowing back and forth through the economic pathways of commerce and government. We are intrinsically interconnected with each other economically. How we act with our money has an impact. When and where we spend our money affects the economic system. The economy, like a large organism, can be strong and thriving or it can be weak and depressed. All of us are affected by the health of the economy.

We also have considerable power individually and collectively by the way in which we spend our money. The money we spend is a vote for that particular product or service. We have the power to strengthen or weaken the different businesses, political parties, special interest groups and so on, depending on where we choose to spend our money. This individual economic power is often overlooked, but is truly an example of the impact that we can have as individuals.

Our economic interconnection now reaches beyond just our own country. It has an impact on the entire world economic market. How each country acts economically can have large and far-reaching effects on the world economy. We now truly live in a global economic village and the money that we spend today ends up on the other side of the world tomorrow. Our individual economic actions have global impact.

There is political interconnection.

Politics is a network of its own and can be seen everywhere. The slogan of our time is "politically correct" and it seems like any action or inaction that we make has political implications. These days it is hard not to be political. We are political even when we choose not to be. Politics is a system based on ideals, agendas, influence, obligation, money, political parties, and special interest groups. We often act and believe that our government is something that is separate from us, but it is not. We are the government and it is a part of us. Our participation, or lack of it, has created the government that we have. It is a reflection of what we believe is important, and the direction we choose to go as a people. The legal system that has come from our political process binds us together under a shared framework of checks and balances of government. Under some systems of government, the individual has a lawful avenue through which they may exert their political power in the form of voting. Although many times the individual is not able to participate in every decision that is made, they are able to participate in electing those who do.

These are some of the more overt examples of how we are interconnected, but now, let us go to a more fundamental level of this concept. This is the true basis for our connection to the Universe and the corresponding interconnection that exists between everything. This foundational basis, I feel, is the most revealing and profound.

There is energetic interconnection.

The science of physics is a very primary way of seeing the interconnection of all things and all events. Physics gives us the ability to understand and fundamentally predict how objects and forces interact with each other. This straightforward approach can help us see the Universe and ourselves in a new way.

Everything that we experience is made up of energy. All that is seen and unseen is a form of energy. Energy is the brick and the mortar, the stuff from which all of creation is made. The whole Universe is just one thing–energy. All the diversity that we can see and experience is due to the fact that energy can take form and change form in an infinite number of ways. There is a basic law of physics that states that energy cannot be created nor can it be destroyed. It has always existed and it always will. Only energy's form can be changed. However, we can manipulate energy. For example, we can concentrate it or we can diffuse it. We can change it from one form to another. We can store it up and we can release its power; but whatever we do, we cannot create energy nor can we destroy it. The Universe is energy and therefore is eternal.

One of the ways that energy takes different forms is based on its vibration. Energy sped up in vibration takes the forms of sound, heat, and light. Energy slowed down in vibration takes the forms of gas, liquid, and solid matter. There are also variations of matter. For example, solid matter can be in the form of stone, wood, steel, glass and so on. Some forms of liquid matter are water, oil, and molten steel. Examples of gases are oxygen, water vapor, and methane gas. These varying forms of matter and their characteristic properties are made up of an interaction of atoms with their own unique energetic vibration patterns. Atoms, themselves, are energy systems made up of even smaller energy systems of protons, neutrons, and electrons–which are in turn made up of even smaller particles of energy like quarks. Atoms have the ability to group together with the same type of atoms or they can group together with other types of atoms to form molecules. From these groupings of atoms, multitudes of compounds can be formed, each with their own particular properties. The physical Universe is made up of atoms, which are, at their core, just an energy system. Therefore, when we look at a rock or a tree we are seeing, in essence, a unique energy pattern–a vibration of energy. That rock or tree is made from the same Universal stuff that all things are made of–energy. We are no exception.

Energy is the thread that ties everything together.

Energy is the thread that ties the whole Universe together. It interconnects us with each other and with everything in the Universe. The Universe is one unified sea of energy.

Why is understanding the interconnection of everything so important? It is so important because everything that we are, everything that we do and everything that we experience in life is interconnected and there is an energetic reason for all of it.

There are no extraneous creations.

The Universe does not create or act without purpose. All that we see and experience exists and occurs for a reason. What would be the point of there being someone, something and some event that did not have or serve a purpose? Every cause produces an effect; every effect originates from a cause. Everything exists because of, and as a result, of a relationship it has with everything else. Why is this extremely important fundamental Truth so lacking in our consciousness today? There are many reasons: developmental, cultural, and technological.

We learn to believe in separation.

From the beginning, we learn to "believe" that we are separate from everything else. When a child is born, they come into the world with a few basic behavioral patterns that are instinctual. For example, one instinct is a grasping response that helps the baby hold onto its mother and not fall. Another is a sucking response so the baby can feed right away. There is a crying response to discomfort so they can get the attention of their caregivers and, hopefully, get their needs met. All of these programmed behaviors are in place at birth so that a child has a good chance of survival. Overall, however, human beings have few hardwired or instinctual behaviors. We gain most of our knowledge of the world through learning. At first, all that infants are aware of is themselves. They experience all kinds of sensory input, but have no idea why. Infants experience their mother and everything else as an extension of themselves, their world is just one undifferentiated sensory experience. As they develop, they begin to make connections between cause and effect. For example, crying when they are hungry results in being fed, sucking their thumb makes them feel better. As we mature, we begin to sort out the many experiences that we have in life and build a sense of ourselves and the world we live in. This very basic level of survival is necessary so that when our caregivers are no longer helping us, we can engage in certain behaviors to maintain and protect our physical body. If that were not the case, we would have a whole different experience of life. The perception of being separate is a helpful one. We believe in it because that is what our sensory experiences have told us. It is an understanding that has helped us maintain our physical body in a physical world.

Our culture defines our position in the Universe.

Our culture plays a strong role in how we see the world and our position in it. Where we place ourselves in the big picture varies greatly. As the many civilizations developed, there has been in many cultures a concurrent loss of conscious understanding of the interconnection of everything. This is particularly true in industrialized cultures. However, some cultures have not lost the understanding of interconnection. These cultures have a completely different understanding. They see themselves as an intrinsic part of the natural world and are very conscious of their connection to it. Their value, honor and even reverence for the plants, animals and minerals results in these cultures living quite differently from the cultures that view man as separate from everything else.

Cultures that live with the land tend to have more of a connection to the earth and live in closer harmony with it. They must. If they act in a way that is out of balance, there can be a very quick and direct impact on their lives. If they over-hunt or deplete their natural resources in some way, their livelihood can be threatened quite directly. Native or indigenous cultures have developed and maintained an understanding of themselves as part of the world in which they live.

Industrialization and technological development has pushed aside many of the native cultures and their understandings. Exploration of the world by some of the more "developed" cultures infused and in some cases forced a very different cultural understanding and mind set upon the native or indigenous people.

For them, the land was something to conquer, to overcome, to take control of and harness. They saw themselves has having dominion over the earth and placed nature under them. The wealth of the land was harvested and the riches fed even more industrial and technological development. What was seen as success and advancement only reinforced their belief that they were separate and that their power over nature was real and justified. If they got in a bind here or there, they were able to free themselves and continue on as they had in the past.

Through the industrial and technological development of a large portion of the earth, most of us have moved into a cultural mindset not bound by the need to survive, feed and clothe ourselves. We have developed into a people of commerce and economics. Economics has become the measuring stick for all endeavors that we undertake; profit is the measure of our success. The focus is to minimize economic costs in order to maximize profit. All the other costs are not always accounted for, like loss of habitat, displacement and destruction of cultures, and the physical and mental health of the people. Our economic policies can, and have in many ways, created more and more separation between people and the natural world.

We have advanced ourselves considerably by our ability to create tools. From fire, to the wheel, to the silicon chip, these tools have given us the ability to extend and magnify the power of our physical bodies. These "advancements" have made our lives easier in some ways and much more complicated in other ways. Technology has transformed how we live. We have created a virtual world apart from nature. Today, a large portion of the earth's population does not live in the natural world, but in a world of steel, concrete and glass. The world that man has created for himself often dominates the landscape, and the natural world is set aside in the form of parks and greenbelts. Yet these are little reminders of the past, shadows of where we originally came from. Nature still exists, but every day there is a little less of it. These modern tools, these extensions of ourselves, have increased our power and at the same time distanced us from the natural earth and from each other.

We have adopted separation consciousness.

Over a very short time period, our modern industrialized societies have separated us so much from nature that we have created a perceptual break with it. We see the food neatly packaged in the supermarket, but are largely unaware of the chain of events that brings that food to the grocery store. We live our lives largely cut off from the natural world and have created long chains of events between how we live our lives and the impact that has on the environment. We often do not make the connection between an oil spill in the ocean and the automobile that we drive to the convenience store, but there is a connection between the two.

Many times, we do not want to look at the connections that exist and so we live our lives in denial about many things. A part of us does not want to become aware of our role in the condition of things. We have created a tidy way of compartmentalizing our lives. We think that what "we do over here" does not affect something else over there. We can live our lives out largely unaware and unconcerned about our impact. This separation consciousness can become quite destructive, taking the forms of addiction, abuse, dishonesty, exploitation and greed. Our self-delusion hurts ourselves, others, and our world, and yet we are unable or willing to see the greater Truth and do something about it. We see this in people from all walks of life from the person on the street to our leaders in positions of great power. We all can fall into these traps of self-deception.

The Universe exists because of differences.

We are social beings, yet in spite of this fact, we often struggle to live peacefully and cooperatively with each other. We form groups for several reasons. This takes place on many levels from the school playground to world politics. Groups come together by defining themselves as sharing a common bond, purpose, belief or set of beliefs that differentiates the group from other people or groups. We see all kinds of groups being formed today for various purposes. Some groups are trying to help, some are trying to hurt, some are trying to gain something and other groups are trying to take something away. We are trying to find a connection with each other and, in doing so, often end up creating even more separation and division. There is nothing wrong with finding a connection with something, someone, or some group, but we cannot continue to connect ourselves with some at the expense of disconnecting ourselves from the whole. We must understand the very basis of the Universe—it is one and many at the same time.

Differences are what make the Universe possible. The Universe is one magnificent thing—energy. That energy is expressing itself in as many ways as possible, creating as many different expressions as possible. That is what makes it such a beautiful place. When we look at differences, we are seeing the most extraordinary aspects of the Universe. If we did not have differences, we would not have a Universe. The Universe is held together because of differentiation. It is the interaction of different forces that literally holds it together. The Universe is made up of positive and negative forces; it is made up of matter and anti-matter; it is made up of physical and non-physical energy. The interaction of all the different forces is the glue that holds atoms together, the earth together, and even keeps our planet on its path around the sun. We must come to terms with this reality. This Truth is such a strong component of the Universe, as well as our everyday lives. The very things that we think of as creating separation and division within and among us—the things that makes us different and distinguished from each other—are actually the very things that make the Universe so strong. It is the differences that are holding it together. If there were not differences, the world would be a boring place. In terms of physics it would not even exist! Our differences are our strength. This is true as individuals, as groups, and as a civilization. Different points of view, different life experiences, different interests and different abilities create a network of strength and a deep well of resources.

The Universe is strengthened by differences.

Nothing exists in a vacuum. A particular group cannot exist without something out there from which to differentiate itself. For example, a conservative political party is what it is because it is different from a liberal political party, which is different from a more moderate political party. If they were not different from each other, then what we would really have is just one party. The whole system would be much weaker, and offer us much less in terms of choice. Many would argue that many political parties are much weaker today because they do not differentiate themselves enough. We need to see and realize that the push and pull between groups, between forces, creates the strength of the Universe and the systems that we create.

This Truth does not just apply to the physics of atoms and biology. It also applies to family systems, business systems, and political and governing systems. We need differences and we need each other. We need a free press to investigate and keep us informed. We need the different parties, platforms and branches of government to push and pull among each other. Look at the systems of government that have only one party. What choice is there? Look at what little debate and discussion there is and how little growth takes place. We must embrace diversity, as well as unity. We are different and we are the same. This paradox is the very basis of the Universe. To be and flow in harmony with the Universe, we must allow all forces to work together. Some people have really tried to make this a reality. We have had much success and we have also failed along the way. In order for us to continue to move forward and not squander the gains that we have made, we must find a way to balance harmony with diversity and individuality with unity. The male is not better than the female; both are equal, only different in expression. It is not one ideology vs. another, but each expressing the Universe in different ways. Culture, race, religion, and politics are different expressions of one human family. We can learn so much from each other. The uniqueness of each individual is what makes the whole so full of promise and potential. We cannot have a declaration of independence without a declaration of interdependence.

The Universe is unified differentiation.

We can have differences and still be united. The Universe operates in this way and so can we. It is the positive that holds the negative in place. There are times of darkness and times of light. We would not be able to see if there were only light. It is the contrast between light and dark that makes vision possible. Life itself is all about color and contrast.

By focusing ourselves so much on the aspects of the Universe that are different, we can lose sight of the fact that these same aspects are also binding it together. From the many influences in our development, culture, technology, we have built an understanding that we are in the Universe but are not connected to it in a real or substantive way. We can feel that we have connections to family, school, job, politics, clubs, and other groups. Those are real connections and are an important part of our lives. There remains, however, a lack of full conscious understanding of just how profoundly we are connected to everyone and everything. Below the surface of our lives there is a very real energetic connection that we all have with the Universe and each other.

We create the world we live in.

This goes beyond just a perceptual reality. It is through our ability and power, as we will see later on in The Second Law of Truth that we literally create the world we live in and that is largely what we have done. We have believed that we are disconnected from the Universe and it has gone along with us and "pretended" that this was the case. The Universe is so responsive and interactive that it helps us to create a complete virtual world with all kinds of props and experiences that will mirror back to us just what we believe it is. The Universe does this so well that we can get so lost in the experience we reach the point of deceiving ourselves from knowing or remembering the greater Truth.

Behind the illusion is the Truth of the Universe.

Whatever we believe and whatever we create, we cannot, fundamentally, remove ourselves from the Universe. The Universe is patient. It will wait a lifetime, an eternity, for us. It is not in a hurry. It knows there is no time; that even time itself is an illusion. The Universe knows that we cannot go where it is not. We can run and hide but our experience is just make-believe or more precisely "believe and then make." Behind the illusion of separation is the greater Truth of the Universe.

We cannot disconnect from the Universe.

We are very much a part of the Universe–so much so that we cannot, as hard as we might try, break our connection to it. Is our father always our father and our mother always our mother? We can say that they are not. We can turn our back on them. We can reject them and we can disown them. However, everything that we do cannot change the fundamental reality that we came from somewhere, from something. We all have an origin, a source, and it is undeniable. We are from the Universe. It is the womb that gave birth to us. We are made from it, each and everyone of us. There are no exceptions and no mistakes. We cannot leave the Universe behind. We can go into a room and lock the door, but we are still in the house!

We have created the experience of limitation.

The Universe lets us go where we want, there are no limitations. Even when we choose limitation itself, the Universe lets us go there without limitation, allowing us to be the most limited person possible. That is how we got here. We chose to believe in limitation and so we created it. We dove into it so deeply that we forgot who we are. We forgot that who we are is something quite remarkable, that we are really not limited at all. We forgot that we were just exploring the room of limitation and became so carried away with the experience that we forgot from where we came.

The good news is that we can find our way out! We can escape our self-created illusion. We can find the key, unlock the door, and walk out of the room of limitation. The Laws of Truth are keys that can unlock the doors between us and the Universe.

Everything is interconnected, no exceptions.

Many belief systems have come closer to the understanding that we are interconnected with each other and the Universe. However, so often, the understanding remains at a conceptual or philosophical level and does not realize the true "energetic" reality of our interconnection. Many times, within some understandings of interconnectedness, there are misconceptions or exceptions. One example is believing that we are connected, except with that group over there, or that person over there, or that thing. The Universe does not leave anyone or anything out. It is inclusive of all that is within it. There is nothing that is outside the Universe. It is one thing and everything is within it.

Reality is more than just the physical.

To gain a more expanded understanding of just how powerful and real our connection to the Universe is, we must expand our understanding of the reality of our existence. There is more to it than what we can see and touch on a physical level. We identify so strongly with our physicality that we do not think of ourselves as being anything more. Yet, who we are is so much more than what we are on a physical level. Our beliefs, thoughts and feelings are what define and direct us. These aspects of our beings make each one of us a unique expression of the Universe. This is something that cannot be seen, and yet it is our experiential reality. Our consciousness is us. It has everything to do with who we are as a human being. Consciousness is invisible; it does not have physicality. It is energy in a form that is not visible. We have a body (physical structure) and within our bodies is a brain that we think of as the place where our mind resides. Yet our mind, our consciousness, is more that just a physical thing. Our consciousness is energy in a form that is non-physical in nature.

One way to think of this is to use a radio broadcast as an analogy. Radio broadcast signals are sent out from a transmitting antenna and they travel over great distances. They are constantly bombarding us, but in order to hear them physically, we need a radio. A radio is a physical device that is able to convert the invisible electro-magnetic energy of a radio signal into a physically audible sound that we can hear. The radio itself does not create the radio signal. The signal is coming from the transmitter. The radio is only transforming the energy from one form to another. We could think of our bodies as doing the same. Like a radio, our bodies are a physical device that is able to transform energy from one form to another. It makes consciousness a physical reality, something that we can experience in our physical body. The energy of our consciousness is transformed into a form of energy that can be expressed physically into actions, spoken words, and feelings.

Our body is also able to take physical reality and make it a conscious experience. Awareness of the physical world is made conscious by our body's ability to transform energy. Our senses receive energy in various forms: light, sound, touch, taste and smell. That energy is transformed and processed in our brains, enabling us to experience the physical world consciously. We can think of the body as a transformer of energy from one form to another. We can also take thoughts and emotions, which are energy that is non-physical, and make them into something that *"is"* physical. Through our minds and bodies we are able to transform the energy of our consciousness into physical forms of spoken or written words, physical movements, music, art, gestures, dance, etc. Physical energy is transformed into consciousness and consciousness is transformed into physical energy.

We are multi-energetic beings.

We are made up of energy that is multidimensional. Not only does our own energy exist on a physical dimension, we are also energy on a non-physical dimension as well. The energy of our totality exists in more than one way. We could use the technology that we have today and look at ourselves in different ways. For example, using photography, we can capture the reflected light that our body gives off. We can also take an X-ray of our body and see an image created from variations in the X-ray energy that is able to pass through our body. Another kind of image can be constructed by using Magnetic Resonance Imagery (M.R.I.), to see the energy that is released when our body is pulsed with a strong magnetic field. There are scans that can be done using our imaging technology that would reveal the different areas of the brain that are activated for different mental tasks. Each modality that we choose is a way of seeing the energy of ourselves in a different form.

However, we are also made up of forms of energy that we have not yet developed the technology to physically measure or quantify. We can assess and infer, indirectly, personality and intelligence through testing and other means, but it does not reveal the wholeness of who we are. We have not yet been able to measure, assess or even recreate the "full reality" of our consciousness, the totality of our human experience.

There are un-measurable aspects of our beings.

We are still working on understanding our physical nature and have barely begun to explore the aspects of ourselves that are non-physical. We have developed many ways to see and measure our physical nature, but those parts of us that are not physical are much more elusive and difficult to quantify. In fact, even trying to measure them physically is rather useless. It would be like trying to detect radio waves by holding our finger in the air. We may even exist energetically in many more ways than we can begin to imagine.

Most of the Universe is anti-matter.

Science has been able to determine that there are other forms of energy outside of what we would call "tangible physical matter"–that which can be measured directly. We are capable of measuring many forms of non-visible energy like radio waves or x-rays by using instruments. This is because, even though these forms of energy are not physical, they still have some detectable attributes. However, beyond even this type of energy, we have determined that there is a whole different type of energy. In fact, we have discovered that the majority of the Universe is primarily made up of this different form of energy, which is called anti-matter. Matter, the aspects of the Universe that we can see directly, measure in some way, or detect with instruments, composes only about 30% of the total Universe. That leaves the majority of the Universe, 70%, being made up of this so-called anti-matter. Anti-matter is interesting, because it cannot be detected directly, its existence must be inferred. We know that it is there by what it does to the forms of energy that we can measure and detect. When matter collides with anti-matter they annihilate each other, leaving only pure energy. Even though it is not tangible, anti-matter is a very real and powerful part of the Universe.

We can only see and touch a fraction of the Universe.

We identify so strongly with what we can see, feel and touch, and yet the majority of the Universe is made up of something that is beyond those senses. This is a powerful Truth of the Universe. The majority of the Universe is intangible and un-measurable beyond our ability to see, touch and feel. We have grounded ourselves so much in the physical world that it is important to take stock in the very structure of the Universe and see how much of it is out there. We are seeing and sensing only a fraction of the Universe directly. We often see our world and ourselves as only being "so much." The Universe is vast and diverse and filled with richness. Those intangible places in the Universe, its largest portions, we know little about. They are beyond the physical, beyond what we can see and touch, and they are mysterious, immense and magnificent.

We are like the Universe itself.

We are not outside the Universe or removed from it. We are a part of and very much connected to it. The Universe is energy in many forms. It would be logical to conclude, that as beings made up of energy, we also have aspects of ourselves that mirror or pattern themselves like the Universe itself. We do have aspects of ourselves that are beyond the physical, beyond our capability to measure directly. The richness of humankind's experience only reinforces this idea. We can, and have, expanded ourselves beyond the physical. We have learned to travel beyond the limits of our bodies. We explore the heavens and dive deep within the atom, exploring and discovering the infinitely largeness and smallness of the Universe itself. Everything that we experience–art, science, music, literature and more– we experience nowhere else but within our being, within our consciousness. Everything that we are comes from that place, that non-physical realm of consciousness.

We are energetic beings.

When we think of ourselves as only a physical being, we are seeing only the smallest part of ourselves and ignoring the rest. We are physical and non-physical beings. We are made of energy. Our body is energy in one form and our consciousness is energy in another. The totality of who we are is energy manifesting in different forms.

This is true of the Universe as a whole. It is also energy manifesting in different forms, some of it physical and some non-physical, some of it tangible and some intangible. Even though we may see ourselves as physical beings, a more complete description would be that we are energetic beings. One portion of our energy exists in our physical body in a physical dimension and a portion of our energy is transcending the physical and exists in the non-physical dimensions of the Universe.

Where there is no physicality, there is no limitation.

Why is it so important to be conscious of the non-physical aspects of ourselves and of the Universe? It is important because where there is no physicality, there are no boundaries or physical limitations. As energetic beings, a portion of ourselves is not bound to the limits of the physical dimension. Yes, we have bodies, but our bodies are just one dimension of ourselves. I believe the major energetic portion of each one of us is non-physical in nature. That portion is many times larger and more powerful than what constitutes us on just a physical level.

We can limit ourselves to a small part of reality.

There has been a growing movement in our cultural "mindset" towards defining reality to just what science can validate through measurement. Many of us have bought into this. So much so, that we have in many ways ignored, denied, and even turned our backs on the "un-explainable." However, there is a very important Truth that we may have overlooked or thought was not significant, a Truth that even our scientists are validating is very real– there is a vast and powerful part of the Universe that is literally beyond measure!

We can expand into the larger part of ourselves.

My desire is for us to expand the notion of who we are. We can get so caught up in our everyday reality that we forget, lose perspective, and never expand beyond it. We are made of the same energy of which the whole Universe is made. If we believe in only that which is physical, we are only using a fraction of our energy, the fraction that is tangible. We are ignoring and putting aside the largest part of our being, that which is intangible and yet many, many times larger and more powerful.

There are many ways energy connects and interacts with us.

To understand The Laws of Truth, we need to be cognizant of energy and the many forms it takes (some physical and some nonphysical), and expand our understanding of how these energetic forces are able to interact with us. As energetic beings, we are impacted by energy in many ways. Some of those ways can be quite large, like an earthquake, or small, like the chemical reactions within the cells of our bodies that keep us alive. However, forces that are not so apparent or tangible can also influence us.

There are many invisible energetic forces.

Energy is remarkable in that it can take forms that are able to connect with us and affect us through the seemingly emptiness of space.

As described before, objects (trees, rocks, you and me) are made up of energy. Everything is some form of energy. The world we live in is filled with all kinds of physical objects, and between those objects we perceive empty space. Perceptually we see nothing, yet there are forces that are acting on those objects that are holding them in place or moving them about. There are real invisible forces that are present in those perceived empty spaces. Where there seems to be nothing, there is actually much going on. Gravity is one force that is not visible, yet it is very much present in keeping us from flying off into space. We cannot see gravity directly but we can perceive and experience its effect. As an example, we step on a bathroom scale and can readily see a measure of the force of gravity on our body. There is a way that gravitational force is able to invisibly reach through space and connect with our body. It is as if invisible strings reach through space and connect to us and pull us down to the surface of the earth. We do not think about it, but that is exactly what is happening. Invisible energy is connecting to us and has a very real and physical effect on us.

Magnetism is another invisible force. We can hold two magnets close together and feel a strong attracting or repelling force between them, depending how their poles are oriented to each other. There is a simple way to demonstrate magnetic forces. When we scatter metal filings on top of a sheet of paper and then hold a pair of magnets underneath the paper, the metal filings are drawn towards the magnets. As the magnets are drawn apart from each other, underneath the paper, the metal filings are attracted to the magnetic field that is running between the two magnets. In essence, the metal filings trace these curved magnetic field lines that connect the two magnets. The filings reveal the pathways in which the magnetic force makes a connection between the two magnets, a connection that can be felt, but cannot be seen, without the aid of the metal filings.

There is a network of invisible forces.

Not only are objects made of energy, but the space between them is filled with energetic forces. The Universe contains energetic forces that are able to make connections to us through the seemingly emptiness of space. Those connections are not just on one level, but on many different levels and in many different ways. The whole Universe is a network of interconnecting and interacting energetic forces.

Space is a very important part of the Universe.

When we study atoms, we find something very interesting–that there is very little physical matter within them. The major portion is just space. An atom is primarily a force field. We could think of our solar system as a very simplistic model of an atom. Yes, there are some large pieces of matter floating around the sun, but when we look at the whole solar system, we find that a major portion is space. Space, though, is not an empty place. Even though we do not see anything, there is a whole world of energetic activity going on. Within space, there are forces and energetic influences flowing throughout that are creating the very structure of our solar system. Without the space and the energetic forces within it, there would be no structure and everything would collapse in on itself. It is important to be aware that what we see, feel, and experience as physical is primarily space. Space is not empty, but filled with invisible energetic forces.

Matter is an important part of the Universe, but even more important is the space in-between. When we look at everything in our world, we tend to focus on the physical, that which we can see and touch and believe to be real. We can ignore, and even disregard, the space and the non-physical. Space, and all that is within it, is just as real, for it helps make the physical possible. Matter and space interact to create what we experience as reality. We need to expand our conscious understanding of reality and realize that the non-physical reality of the Universe is just as important, if not more important, than what we perceive to be the physical reality.

Energy is able to flow throughout the Universe.

This is a very significant Truth. Energy is able to flow throughout the Universe, through space and through matter. In addition, because everything that we are and everything that we do is fundamentally energy, that energy is able to move and flow throughout a multitude of energetic pathways that exist within the Universe.

The Universe is a G.E.M. (Grand Energetic Matrix).

The Universe is one interconnected energetic field. Think of it as a system or matrix of energetic pathways in which energy can move and flow. Moreover, think of that matrix as one in which every point is connected to every other point in some way. The Universe is a G.E.M., a Grand Energetic Matrix of interconnected pathways in which energy here can flow over there and energy over there can flow over here.

What is fascinating is that the human brain is really just a matrix of interconnections like the Universe itself. Our physical brains are composed of an immense network of pathways made up of neurons. Neurons function like cables that are able to generate electrical impulses and then channel that electrical energy to other neurons. An impulse in one neuron can travel to others, depending upon how that neuron is interconnected. Our brains contain billions and billions of these interconnections. Some neurons have the ability to excite other neurons and some have the ability to inhibit other neurons, creating a complexity within our brain that is literally "mind-boggling."

When we think of the size and scope of the Universe, our ability to comprehend the number of ways the Universe is interconnected is stretched to the limit. It is unfathomable. We all have within us a small version of the Universe itself–the human brain, a complex matrix of interconnections that can do incredible things. Imagine the power of the Universal matrix, one that is of infinite size, complexity and capability.

The Universe is intelligent.

We might be thinking, "How can the Universe be intelligent?" Well, it has all the hardware of a brain, why would it not also have intelligence? It has connections, pathways in which energy can flow in a multitude of ways. The whole structure of the Universe is tied together in a cohesive unit. Nothing is out of place or removed from the whole. Everything that exists within the Universe is there for a

reason and any action or change is a result of some energetic transformation. If everything is a form of energy and energy can flow in a
multitude of ways, then a lot is going on. What we can see and measure is only a fraction of the Universe. If we consider the other 70% of
the Universe, then that larger portion could be playing an even larger
role in how we experience life and what goes on and why things work
the way they do. What we see and experience is only a small part of
the picture. There is a greater portion of the Universe operating behind the scenes. That hidden portion is there for a reason and playing
a part in making the Universe work the way that it does.

Why would there not be some form of intelligence to the system? When we look at life itself, there is something very thoughtful
about how it all works. From the smallest creature to the largest and
most complex, there is evidence of intelligence on some level. Both
a virus and bacteria are able to maintain and procreate, adapt and
change. There is intelligence in ecosystems interacting and adapting
in remarkably intricate and complex ways. The earth is an amalgam
of systems. There are ecosystems–oceanic, geologic, and weather
systems–all interacting and communicating with each other. The
development of this particular planet in our solar system can only
be described as extraordinary, to say the least.

Beyond earth, there is something quite remarkable about how
the stars, solar systems and galaxies are created. They have their own
life cycle, how they take form and, in time- frames beyond comprehension, change into something else. There is such beauty in how,
within the Universe, the transformation of energy is taking place on
so many levels and in so many ways. What is out there is so vast, and

what we see and know is such a tiny part of a picture that is beyond measure.

The Universe holds all consciousness.

Is the Universe conscious? This is the question of all questions. Are we conscious? We would say yes. However, defining consciousness is a struggle. We have used several different criteria, but many have fallen by the wayside. Things like self-awareness, the ability to experience and communicate emotion, have shown up in many non-human species. For a long time we thought only man was conscious and that animals were not. However, through our research and study, we have learned that this distinction is not that clear. We have discovered that several animals like chimpanzees, gorillas and dolphins are able to recognize themselves in a mirror, to communicate in complex ways, and show signs of emotion. Anyone who has cared for or worked with animals has seen them in varied "emotional" states. Many animals, wild and domestic, have exhibited "playful" behavior. Therefore, the line between man and "animal" is not as distinct as we might think. We have the tendency to take our experience and apply it to other things. This is only natural for us to try to use our own frame of reference to understand our world. However, our frame of reference is limited in many ways. Animals may be conscious, but in a different way. Even though their consciousness may not be of a human quality, it is probable that they have some form of consciousness.

Consciousness, on a Universal level, is a challenge to comprehend and understand. It clearly stretches the frame of reference of our own experience. There are some things that we do know that we can put together to help us understand what Universal consciousness might be. We know that the earth is populated by billions of conscious beings and those beings are interconnected on many levels to create a form of global consciousness. We can see this clearly on the levels of culture, education, science, economics and government. We have a rather large interconnected pool of knowledge and resources from a world perspective. On this level, we are able to see how each person's participation grows the conscious understanding of the world we live in. When we put all that together, we have a "global" consciousness, a collective understanding. Now, if we choose to step into the deeper energetic levels of the Universe that we have discussed, it is not hard to see the enormous capacity of knowledge and even awareness that is possible. Energy is able to move and flow throughout the Grand Energetic Matrix and this includes the energy of our consciousness—individually and collectively. When we begin to grasp this, we can see that there are really no boundaries, no separation; that even in consciousness we are interconnected. We tend to think of ourselves as individuals, drawing lines between us, the rest of the world and Universe. When we go to the higher levels of the Universe, those levels beyond the physical, the lines fade away and the separation that we perceive disappears.

The Universe is expressing its potential.

The Universe is quite remarkable. Some see it as intelligent and others see it as just an accident, an interaction of the right elements "randomly" coming together. The Universe is anything but an "accident." The word "accident" contradicts the very basis of the Universe. Everything that is here and out there is, because it can be. What we are seeing is the potential and possibility of the Universe taking form. We, along with everything else, are here because the Universe is expressing itself in the ways that it can. Every space, every niche is being filled with all the energetic possibility and potential that exists.

The Universe is creating time and space and, at the same time, filling it with all that we can and cannot see. It is one unified thing manifesting itself in a multitude of ways. The Universe is just energy, and yet that energy can, and is, taking form in all the varied ways possible. The Universe is not an accident. When we think of an accident, we think of something that is out of place or unexpected; something that has no reason and just happens. The Universe cannot do something without a reason. Reason means connection, a causal link between cause and effect and effect and cause. There is nothing in the Universe that is not connected somehow and in some way. When we flip a coin there is a reason why it lands on its head or on its tail. The shape and movement of our hand generates a velocity, angle and spin that interacts with the density of the air, and so on, to create a complex of energetic influences that come together to create an outcome.

Is the Universe just a simple mechanistic cause and effect place? Are we just biological robots that can be reduced to neural impulse-response interactions? If we isolate a part of anything it may appear to be simple. Even the most complex computer can be dissected into an input/output, on/off binary switching device. Yet when we look at the whole, it is clearly not simple. The Universe is a complex place, and yet it has within it some very basic relationships that build one on another to form systems. All the systems are then interconnected to form the Grand Energetic Matrix.

The Universe has its own way of doing things.

When we look at the whole Universe, there is a cohesive intelligence and consciousness to it. We can have several perspectives of this. We could think of the Universe as a grand mainframe computer, or we can think of it as a Divine Being. Either way, the Universe still works the same; it has its own way of doing things.

We have made great strides in understanding how and why things are the way that they are in the Universe. However, there is so much we do not know. We may not always be able to make sense of it or explain it right now, but if it exists, if it happens, it does so because of the interconnecting and interacting energetic forces of the Universe.

We can expand ourselves into the Universe.

Through our conscious awareness of the Law of Interconnection, we can extend ourselves out into a much bigger arena. That arena is the Universe, which is infinite. We are not an element or a particle separate from the whole. We are part of something that is unlimited and, therefore, through our connection with it, we have access to all that it holds.

We play a part in the Universe.

Nothing is outside the Universe. All is contained within it, from the smallest particle to the largest galaxy. We are not tiny and insignificant aspects of the cosmos, although it may seem that way when we look at the size and scope of the Universe. The smallest part can play the largest role. Remove the right part from a car and it will stop running, or from a plane and it will cease to fly. The smallest movement can trigger a landslide or launch a rocket into space. We think of ourselves as being just so much, yet we larger and more powerful than we can imagine. We have powerful and far-reaching effects because of the very real connection that we have with the Universe. Still, we are largely unaware of our power and its impact. That impact is within our own personal lives and it reaches far beyond. Our world, our Universe, is a much larger place than we can possibly comprehend, and our opportunities and potential can be just as infinite.

Our part is significant in making the Universe what it is.

When I say we "play a part in the Universe," I mean we each play a significant role. We are not bystanders watching the world go by. We are participants. As energetic beings and because of the energetic basis of the Universe, we are plugged into and part of the Grand Energetic Matrix. The energy of the Universe flows into us and we, in turn, express that energy back into the Universe. Each one of us plays a role in expressing the fullness of what is the Universe. This is no small matter. This is a tremendous opportunity and responsibility.

The Universe is not complete without us.

We are aspects of the Universe, each one of us. We make up part of "what is." Therefore, each one of us is valuable and important. The Universe cannot fully express itself without us. If one part is removed, then the Universe would be incomplete and that is not possible! The Universe is always complete! Each one of us plays a role in filling out that completeness. We each play a part in making the Universe everything that it is. There is a portion of its fullness and potential that the Universe holds that can only unfold and be realized through each one of us.

The Universe is actually relying on us to do our part. Every person carries within themselves a potential, an aspect, of the Universe that is waiting to be expressed, much like a small seed of a great tree. The seed contains all the potential of the tree, but it is yet to be realized or manifested into the full expression of a mature tree. Likewise, each of us holds a unique potential that plays a part in expressing the full potential of what the Universe contains. When we express ourselves fully and completely we are bringing forth the promise that the Universe holds into this reality, this human experience.

Everyone on this planet is here for a reason, here for the Universe, here for all of us, and here for themselves. We must realize and value the significance of this.

Our power is our birthright.

This ability to express the Universe through ourselves is the source of our power. What is more powerful than the Universe? Nothing! Astonishingly, each one of us is made from it and has been given the ability to express it through our beings. This ability does not just belong to a few. It is the birthright of every single one of us. The Universe has given us this gift regardless of our background, heritage, and circumstances, physical or mental capability. This is a gift that we cannot lose or give away. This gift belongs to everyone. We can decide to put it aside, keep it locked up and choose not to use it, but our power is always there for us, it is always a part of us. It is who we are.

Many people lack awareness, many lack willingness and many are just afraid, but throughout history we have seen examples of people who have stepped into their power. There are people who have been able to express it quite fully in their lives. Even in our present day current affairs, there are plenty of examples of individual people having great impact. It has happened, and is happening, throughout the world; individuals are making a difference. We have seen and heard of many examples of this use of power.

Power comes in many forms.

The Universe is the source of all power. We have been given this incredible gift, which is access to its power. We have also been given the gift of free will, the choice of how to use it. Man has often misused this power, choosing to use it to destroy, to conquer and to obtain, rather than to heal, to build and to share. Man's use of power is often a distortion and at odds with the natural flow of the Universe. The power of the Universe is immense. It can be used wisely and it can be misused. The atomic bomb is a grave example of man's misuse of Universal power. Our commercial media intentionally tries to grab our attention with the dramatic and the sensational. As a result, we have a tendency to focus on the more overt and physical examples of power. We often think of physical power, economic power, political or military power, but all power is energy and therefore comes in many forms.

There is a higher power, a power that is different. It transcends the dimensions of physicality. Often that is where the higher power has the most impact, creating the most change, working invisibly behind the scenes initially. Then it begins spilling over, quite dramatically at times, into the physical world.

Some of the most powerful people in history initially looked and appeared on the surface to have very little physical, economic, or political power. Examples would be Mahatma Gandhi, Mother Theresa and Nelson Mandela. These beings and many other powerful people have been able to access a higher level of power and from it gain the ability to transcend the physical. This higher power effected enormous change. They did what many had tried to do but had failed at by using other means. Their power came from another place and was able to reach us in a different way than the physical. When this higher power of the Universe flows through us it can capture hearts, open minds and free spirits.

Many times when we are challenged by the physical world, we are forced to find this source of power, to discover a power beyond the physical that we did not know was there, but was. We are often like Dorothy in *The Wizard of Oz* discovering that we had the power all along. We were searching outside of ourselves and in the end, we found our power from within.

There is no insignificance in the Universe.

We are prone to see and focus on the larger, more significant, examples of power. However, the world is what it is by the small things that we do. Each of us contributes to the collective experience that we all have. We affect others and they affect us. A kind word, a pat on the back, can change someone's day. We have all heard this before, but these things must be seen in a different light. The energy of any action is real and has an affect that is equally so. Within any interaction, large or small, an energetic pulse travels throughout the Universe. The physical world can deceive us—we can be taken in by the large and underestimate the small.

There are no insignificant parts and there are no insignificant people. Everyone matters and everyone is contributing, consciously or not. Everything that we are and everything that we do has an impact on the Universe, literally, powerfully and with far-reaching effect. We are each here for a reason and have a job to do. We each have a tremendous capability, opportunity and responsibility to contribute not only to creating and shaping our own lives, but contributing to the lives of everyone else. We have been given the keys to something that is nothing less than extraordinary. What we do with them is up to us. We have the choice to pick up the keys and unlock the door to the amazing creative power and potential within us.

Everything serves a purpose and plays a role.

Everything, from the largest to the seemingly most insignificant, is there for a purpose. If the Universe is a system of energetic relationships and there is a fundamental interconnection between them, then there is a reason for each and every element and each and every part. Just like a car is a system of parts that is connected to each other and work and relate to each other in a way that serves a purpose.

The Interconnection of the Universe is working for us.

Our lives are no different. The many parts work, or may appear not to work, because of how they interconnect. Our families, our neighbors, our coworkers, our communities and so on make up a network of human interconnections that create a social network for us. How we interact and relate to them and how they relate to us makes up a large part of how we experience our lives.

I want us to look beyond our own apparent social networks and realize that we are connected to everyone and everything on this planet. The person on the street that we do not know is still connected to us in some way. We could say that they share the fact that we are both from the same city or state or country. Maybe they have some other common thread; they might like the same kind of music or political party. There always seems to be something that we can find in another person, something to connect to and share some understanding or similarity. Perhaps we are both parents raising a child or we just lost a close friend. Our lives are filled with all kinds of experiences and we have all kinds of beliefs and desires. When we are able to share who we are with someone else, we often find common ground and understanding with each other. However, I want us to go even further. We could say that we connect with each other because we all share a basic human condition with everyone on this planet because we are all having a human experience. This is clearly a level of interconnection that is true and real.

Yet, I want us to go deeper still, beyond looking at our interconnection from just a biological or social level, to a place of seeing that we are connected to each other on a very fundamental level of energy. Energy is the fundamental universal force that flows through all of us and through everything. It flows through all the people of the earth and binds us together. This binding together is not just social, political or biological. It is energetic. Not only does this energy create all the interconnection that we can see, but it also creates all the interconnection that we cannot see. If most of the energy of the Universe is non-physical, then we are sharing a vast amount of energy that is a reality of its own. What we can see and touch is only a fraction of the total Universe. We are connected to each other and communicating with each other in this other arena or reality that is beyond the physical, and it is immense and powerful. Therefore, when we see someone on the street that we might not be able to visibly make a connection with or share some understanding with, we must realize that there is still a connection. When we build this understanding, this consciousness of The Law of Interconnection, we begin to see the world differently. We are able to see that how we are and how we act has a very real impact on the rest of the Universe.

We live in a Universal energetic village.

Nothing is isolated from us. We are all in the same boat, in the same energetic sea. If a child is in a family that has an undercurrent of abuse that is not directly experienced or witnessed by the child, the child is still impacted by it. The violence that exists in our neighborhoods, in our communities, in our countries affects all of us. Even the violence on the other side of the world affects us. The terrorist attack on the United States World Trade Center was an attack on the world. It has had, and will have, a profound and lasting affect on everyone. The energy of that event has traveled around the world, into the homes and lives of all of us, and shaken us to our foundations. The large events obviously have impact, but so do the small ones. Everything has energy to it–from a thought, to a look, to a gesture–and we are impacted by it, consciously or not. We cannot ignore the energy of all things that we initiate and create in our lives and the things created in the lives of everyone else. We live in a global energetic village.

We are not disconnected, but interconnected. When we realize that and then believe, feel and act in alignment with the Universe, the world that we create will work because we are creating a world that flows with the forces of the Universe. We have created many wondrous things and built civilizations. We have established remarkable networks of commerce and government. Yet, the road we have chosen towards progress and development has had many costs. That cost has been weighed as being worth the benefit, but is the cost/benefit equation out of balance? Is the planet losing its balance? Are our lives losing their balance? We seem to keep creating some of the same problems that humankind has had since the beginning of time, as well as new ones.

How we are on the inside affects everything.

To change our course, we must realize that everything that we are and everything that we do affects the whole. It is not just how we act, more importantly it is how we are. What is going on in the inside, affects the outside. We need to place our focus on what is going on behind the scenes. Because who we are on the inside, what we believe determines the reality that we experience.

We spend so much time and energy trying to change things out there, ignoring or discounting what we hold within us. It is our consciousness that needs our attention. What we believe, our Truth is what has the most power to make changes in our lives. In Chapter 2, we will learn how we can choose and direct the powerful energy of our consciousness and how the Universe will respond to us.

II.
THE SECOND LAW OF TRUTH

OUR ENERGY IS REFLECTED BACK
TO US BY THE UNIVERSE

EVERYTHING THAT WE ARE, everything that we experience is fundamentally energy. This is true of that which makes us most human, which is our mind, our ability to have consciousness. The beliefs, emotions and thoughts that we have are forms of energy and, because of that, they move, flow, and interact with everything else like all energy does. This energy of our consciousness interacts with the Universe because we are interconnected with it. The Universe responds to our energy and reflects back to us energy that is similar or complimentary to our energy pattern. This energy reflected back to us by the Universe can take many forms, such as people, experiences and things.

Through conscious choice, we can choose what we are telling the Universe by our energy pattern and, in so doing, we can create, shape and direct our experience of the Universe. This remarkable ability and the power it offers us are available to those who are willing to choose it. However, in order to have this power to shape our experience of the Universe, we must learn more about ourselves. We need to learn that what we hold in our consciousness, tells the Universe in a very powerful way what we want to experience.

We transmit energy by our beliefs, emotions, thoughts and actions.

Our beliefs, emotions, thoughts and actions are the characteristic patterns of energy that we are transmitting into the Universe. What we hold within us is as important as the actions we take. Those actions come from what we believe, feel, and think about ourselves and the world we live in. Of these aspects of consciousness, it is our beliefs that need our focus and attention, because they are the most powerful forms of energy that we can choose to hold and transmit into the Universe. This is a powerful Truth and one that needs to be looked at in detail.

Beliefs differ from thoughts. Thoughts are ideas that have not taken root in our belief system. This is an important distinction. We can have a thought but it does not have as large of an energetic effect as a belief until we anchor it to our being by believing in it. We can think of thoughts as energy forms that are moving and flowing around. They can come into our consciousness and can just as easily flow out. We can be aware of the thoughts and still not be invested in them. A thought really takes hold when we believe in it. When we make a thought a Truth, by believing in it, it then becomes part of us and our belief system is restructured to include it. Not only is our belief system altered but, as we will see, so is our reality.

Our Truth is our reality.

When we believe in something, we believe it to be the Truth. That Truth is an understanding of what we hold to be real and reliable.

A Truth is something we can depend on in the present and in the future. We refer to it; we make decisions and choose courses of action on what we believe. Our beliefs have the final say; they hold a tremendous position of power in our consciousness. Everyone's Truth is their own. We all have a unique view of ourselves and the world, and likewise, a unique belief system of what Truth is. There are many, many Truths within the Universe. The Truth, The Truth of the Universe, is made up of all those Truths.

There is a hierarchy of energy in our consciousness.

Beliefs are energy and, as discussed before, there are differences in the vibratory rate of energy. For example, energy in the form of x-rays is of a higher vibration than energy in the form of light. In turn, light energy is of a higher vibration than sound energy and so on. We can think of all energy as existing on a spectrum of varying degrees of vibration. Because beliefs, emotions and thoughts are also energy, they also differ in their vibratory rate. Beliefs are of higher vibration than emotions, and emotions are of a higher vibration than thoughts. When we classify these aspects of our human consciousness as energy, we can understand them in a new way. Because there is an energetic hierarchy between beliefs, emotions and thoughts, we can use this to help us understand the varying degrees of impact and interaction they have on us.

Our beliefs are one of the highest forms
of energy in our consciousness.

Our Beliefs have great impact on us and are a source of tremendous power in our lives. It is through our beliefs that we organize, understand and structure our reality. This is the real place of power in human consciousness and the place where change can result in the most dramatic of results. The beliefs that we hold as individuals and as a collective group literally create our reality.

Beliefs are the windows through which we view our world. Some people have large windows and some people have small ones. Sometimes the windows are just on one side of the house and we can only see in one direction, missing the world that is on the other sides of the house. Sometimes the windows get dirty and we do not realize it, and sometimes they just get boarded up. To grow and expand in consciousness, we need to work towards making our windows larger and larger and building them in all directions so that we can envision all that there is. When the time comes to leave the house, we will step out in the open and then be able to see all that there is without anything obstructing our view.

Because our beliefs have so much power, we need to take a close look at how they are created and how they can shape our perceptions and color our experiences in life.

We filter our experiences through our beliefs.

It is through our beliefs that we filter our experiences in life. That is why our first experience with something is often the most profound–

we have little or no preconceptions about it. Without preconceptions, which are forms of belief, we are able to experience something fully, purely, without distortion. The experience is not altered by our previous experience with it or what others have told us about it. But, two people can be subjected to the exact experience and each will have their own interpretation of it. Why is that? It is primarily a product of what they believe about the world, about themselves and about that experience.

We build a belief system about the world.

We are individuals because we each have a unique belief system or Truth. We are a complex set of beliefs that are built one-by-one from the beginning of our first experiences as children. As we grow and mature, we construct our own version of the world in our consciousness. In the beginning, it is primarily a cause-and-effect sensory investigation of life. However, as we learn to use language we are able to receive information from others. Language allows us to learn about the world indirectly. It is through the medium of language that we are able to pass on our experiences as well as what we have learned about the world to our children. We learn a lot about life through this process of acquiring information secondhand. Much of what we believe comes from the knowledge of others.

A large portion of what we believe about reality, what we consider Truth, we have not experienced directly.

Direct experience is not always trustworthy.

Our most direct knowledge about the world comes from our own personal experience. It is what we often hold to be the most real for us. However, direct experience is not always as reliable as we might think. There have been scientific experiments that have shown that a whole group of people can interpret the very same-shared experience in a variety of ways. In fact, eyewitness testimony is often inaccurate and our memory and ability to recall an experience is very susceptible to influence. Additionally our perceptions can change and distort over time. Distortions of an experience can be the result of many factors: limitations in physical perception, our ability to remember, our emotional response to the situation, previous experiences, attitudes, preconceptions, and so on.

Many of our beliefs are acquired from others.

As children, we are very observant and learn through imitation. Children will many times pick up a belief because they see others expressing it, especially if it is a "significant" person in their life. Children learn much about the world through observation and imitation. "If others believe this, it must be true" and they strive to incorporate as much as they can about the world in as many ways as they can and they carry this "Truth" forward into life, often without much thought. This happens because when we are young we have not yet developed the ability to analyze and engage in critical thinking or use logic to test those beliefs. Later on in adulthood, the experiences that we have in life either support that training or contradict it. However, because much of what we believe about the world comes from such a young and influential age, our early training is very resistant to change and even to challenge from conflicting experience, logic or rational analysis. Those early beliefs stand like monuments from an age long past. Many times, their meaning is no longer relevant, their validity is questionable, and yet we may never think to ask: "Why do I believe that?" We hold on to these beliefs and sometimes it takes quite an event or someone else's observations to get our attention that a belief is out of alignment with our goals and not supportive or congruent with whom we want to be.

We can define ourselves based on opinions of others.

We also build a belief structure about ourselves that comes from others. As social beings, we can be strongly influenced by the opinions of other people, especially those who are important to us like our family, friends, and teachers. Other people can be helpful in providing us with feedback, but sometimes their feedback is not always accurate, honest or constructive. Social pressure and the approval of others can be very influential and we can become too dependent on this external source of information, defining ourselves more on the opinions of others than on our own judgment. We can rely too heavily on external validation and spend our lives trying to live up to expectations of others. Expectations can be positive or negative. We can be expected to succeed and we can be expected to fail. However, the ultimate authority lies in our own hands. We are the ones who must define who we are and what our Truth is, based on what we believe it to be.

We often have false beliefs.

Our Truth is our responsibility. What we believe is vitally important and yet, for many of the reasons just discussed, our beliefs can be inaccurate and downright faulty. Much of our struggle in life is largely a result of false beliefs about ourselves, about others and about the world. False beliefs can be deeply rooted and their validity is often never challenged nor their origins traced to their source. So much emotional and psychological pain and resulting dysfunctional behavior often comes from holding onto inaccurate beliefs. Anxiety, fears, phobias, self-loathing and depression are so often caused by distortions of reality. The focus of the mental health profession is to help correct those misperceptions, especially when they begin to interfere with one's ability to function in life. There can be much effort, time and energy expended in undoing the distortions, but it is vital that we do so. If we do not, then these distortions are carried with us and continue to create unhealthy ways of responding to life. We can all have varying degrees of misperceptions and distortions about reality. Great or small, they affect us in some way, limiting our ability to know and experience life fully.

Our belief system needs to be a work in progress.

I bring this up so that we might begin to take a good hard look at what we believe and where those beliefs are coming from. What we believe about ourselves and the world we live in can be accurate, useful and healthy. Likewise, much of what we hold to be Truth can also be false, dysfunctional, and crippling. It is imperative that we look very carefully at our belief system. It is our framework; it is who we are as a person. However, like any framework, each part needs to be working to support the whole. Each belief that we hold needs to be carrying its weight. Beliefs are power and that power can work for us or against us. We can have positive supporting beliefs in one area and have negative crippling ones in another. The saying, "A chain is only as strong as its weakest link," applies here because the crippling beliefs that we hold within us can disable the positive ones and our progress in life can grind to a halt.

Our goal to a healthy and productive life is to hold within us the best version of reality that we can. It is an ongoing process of constantly working to maintain that which works, and modifying and improving upon that, which does not. The model of the world that we hold within us needs to be a work in progress. We must actively strive to be conscious of what we believe about ourselves and the world we live in. To make changes in ourselves and how we experience the world, we must focus on our beliefs because of the tremendous power they have in our lives. Changing our beliefs to match our desires will support and facilitate that which we want to bring into our lives.

Beliefs are more than understandings—
they are energetic patterns.

To be powerful and effective people, we need to have powerful and effective beliefs. We must have a belief structure that is strong and finely tuned to our goals. Our success in whatever we choose to pursue in life absolutely depends on it. However, beliefs are more than just statements or understandings that guide our actions or lead us toward our goals. They are energetic patterns. Our beliefs are the very powerful way that we transmit the energy of our consciousness into the Universe. Consciousness is not bound or limited and our beliefs are not confined to just our own consciousness.

We transmit an energy signal out to the Universe.

Our beliefs are one of the most powerful ways that we transmit energy out into the Universe, but we also give off energy by what we feel, by our thoughts and by our actions. Think of it as a collective energetic broadcast that is being transmitted out into the Universe.

Our total energetic transmission interacts with the energy of the Universe and the Universe in turn responds to our energetic broadcast and mirrors back to us what we are sending out.

*We are having a dynamic energetic
interaction with the Universe.*

Our energy is not static. It is flowing out from us into the Universe and the energy of the Universe is flowing back to us through all the interconnections that exist within the Universe. We are constantly interacting with the Universe and it, in turn, is interacting with us. Conscious or not, our connection to the Universe exists and an energetic interaction is taking place.

An analogy is to imagine that we are standing on the edge of a canyon and we yell or make a sound. The sound, which is a form of energy, goes out and has a characteristic pattern of vibration in the form of sound waves. Those waves hit the walls of the canyon and then are reflected back to us in the form of an echo. What is most noticeable is the delay of the returning sound waves. There is also sometimes a reverberation of the sound as it bounces around and hits the various surfaces of the canyon and is reflected back to us in various directions. There is often a change in the character of the sound as it interacts with the contours and other characteristics of the canyon. Likewise, the Universe reflects back to us what we are sending out. It may be delayed, it may come back to us from a different direction, and it may be of a different quality, but still the energy will be reflected back to us in some way and in some form.

Our experience in life is a reflection of who we are.

What we experience in life is an echo, a reflection of what we are transmitting or sending out into the Universe. The Universe is constantly reflecting back to us what we believe, feel and think about ourselves and our world. To know ourselves better, we need only to look around us. Our family, our friends, our jobs, where we live, the experiences we have and even the objects that we own are a reflection of the energy of who we are. In essence, then, we are co-creators of our world. From all energy, all is created.

We do not create energy, but we take it in and we channel it out and what we channel out into the Universe is the energy of our beliefs, emotions, thoughts and actions. Everything that we believe, feel and do in life creates an energetic pattern, a frequency that we transmit out to the Universe. In turn, everything in the Universe that matches, or is similar enough to our energy signal, tunes into our signal and shows up in our lives. The people, experiences, and things that come into our lives do so because they match who we are energetically.

Simply put: Like energy is drawn to like energy.

If, for example, we send out the energy of abundance, we will draw to us people that are abundant, experiences that are abundant and our physical world will reflect abundance. If, on the other hand, we send out the energy of lack of abundance, we will draw to us people that lack abundance, experiences that lack abundance, and our physical world will be lacking in abundance.

We can tune into any part of the Universe we want.

We can tune our energetic signal to any channel we want. It is a function of what we believe, feel, think and how we act. We can be on the abundance channel or the lack channel, the success channel or the failure channel, the knowledge channel or the ignorance channel. Each channel carries with it a whole world of people, experiences, and things that share that particular energetic pattern.

The Universe is full of a multitude of different energetic channels. Like the energy spectrum that we talked about previously, we can also think of all energetic channels as existing on a spectrum as well. Each channel is, in a sense, a separate or distinct place within the Universe that has its own particular characteristic properties. There are many different channels or places in the Universe and we have the ability to tune into them and experience them. In essence, that is what we are doing right now. We have each tuned into a particular energetic place in the Universe, consciously or not. At all times, we are dynamically telling the Universe where we want to be, where we want to reside within it. That is how powerful we are, how capable we are, and that is how much potential we have. We have the power, the ability and the potential to place ourselves wherever we choose.

We are in a powerful place.

We have placed ourselves here in this three dimensional earth-based reality. Is this a mistake? Did we make a wrong turn? I do not believe so. We are powerful beings and this is a powerful place. There are no accidents and no extraneous or meaningless events or experiences. There is no place identical to earth anywhere else in the Universe. The earth is a unique place full of richness in opportunity, experience and growth. We have each chosen to be here, chosen to experience this life in this part of the Universe. However, even here, there is a wide range of experiences and we have the ability to fine-tune our belief systems and draw to us particular aspects of what this dimension, this place in the Universe, has to offer. Even within each of our own unique individual situations, we can choose to experience them in different ways. We can adjust the way we experience life by adjusting our beliefs. We can tune into and experience an infinite range of possibility that exists within us and within our place in the Universe.

The Universe is always telling us who we are.

Another way to understand this process is to see the Universe as an input/output system, like a grand computer. It is working all the time, to show us who we are, in a perfect way, whether we are conscious of it or not. The energy of every belief, feeling, thought and action that we generate is an energetic input message going into the G.E.M. (Grand Energetic Matrix) or Universe, and the Universe is calculating a perfect way to respond to our input.

We can transmit a mixed signal.

Many times our lives are confusing, conflicted and chaotic. This is because we often broadcast a variety of different energetic messages to the Universe. The Universe, in turn, reflects back to us a mixture of different realities. It is like we are tuning into many different stations at the same time. Some channels are turned up very loud and dominate our attention and lives, while others murmur in the background. The energy signal that we transmit out into the Universe can be very "interesting" to say the least. As complicated, conflicted, and contradicting our beliefs are, so is our signal, which is transmitted to the Universe.

We can be transmitting a lot of static and the Universe can only respond in kind. It is the old computer programming saying "garbage in, garbage out." If our lives are a mess, we need to look at what we are telling the Universe by our energy signal. If we have a belief system that is in disarray and cluttered with contradiction and conflict, then our experiences in life are going to mirror those beliefs.

We must tell the Universe what we want.

If we like who we are and what we are experiencing, then I suggest that we continue to be who we are. We can continue to believe what we believe, feel and act as we have been acting. If we do not like what we are experiencing in life and want to have things change, then we must look at what we are telling the Universe with our beliefs.

It is that simple and that powerful. We are powerful beings and we have the ability to co-create what we want in our lives with the help of the Universe. To improve our lives, we must look at what we are telling the Universe by our energetic signal and, most importantly, by our beliefs. We must clean up our signal and eliminate the static. First, let go of the beliefs that contradict and weaken us, that make our direction and purpose unclear. Second, identify the beliefs that we want to keep, that support who we want to be and what we want to experience and have in life. Third, adopt, develop and enhance beliefs in the areas of our life that need help. Through these efforts, we will end up with a concise, consistent and powerful message of what we desire for ourselves and our world.

The Universe will respond to our new energetic signal, beginning right away to reflect back to us in as many ways that it can, what we are telling it with our new beliefs. Those new beliefs will allow us to experience new feelings, thoughts and if we choose to take new actions.

We have the tools to build the life and world we desire.

Our beliefs are powerful tools that we have at our fingertips to build the life and the world that we desire. We have always had these tools, but now we have a greater understanding of their power and potential. We have always played a pivotal role in creating our own life, but now we are gaining greater consciousness of just how much power and responsibility we actually have.

The Universe will work with us.

There is nothing more powerful than the Universe. We have the ability to work consciously with it, and it will work with us. It is a partnership, one of boundless potential. As we gain more and more access to our power by incorporating more and more powerful beliefs, the Universe will reflect back to us more and more powerful aspects of what it contains. The more we claim our power by believing that we have it, the more power the Universe will turn over to us. It is no accident that powerful people draw other powerful people to them as well as powerful opportunities and powerful experiences. The Universe is always there for us—in every moment, 100%, supporting us in who we believe we are.

We have reached a powerful place: conscious awareness.

Consciousness is powerful. We now have the awareness that what we believe is one of the most powerful ways that we communicate with the Universe. We know that it will listen and respond to us. To be conscious of this allows us to use this knowledge to create remarkable changes in our lives. We can actively and intentionally use our ability to communicate with the Universe. It is up to each one of us to choose how to use this knowledge and this power.

III.
THE THIRD LAW OF TRUTH

CHANGE ANYTHING AND WE CHANGE EVERYTHING

TO GROW AND DEVELOP we must change. Change is the very basis of the Universe. It plays a pivotal role in making the Universe work the way that it does, so understanding change is important. Nothing in the Universe is static and yet, we can be deceived into believing just the opposite and we can feel that we are stuck in life. The Third Law of Truth addresses the dynamic power of change and its use as a tool of transformation.

The Third Law of Truth has its basis in the previous two laws that we have discussed, so let us review the laws and relationships that have brought us to this point. In Chapter 1, we learned that the Universe is a Grand Interconnected Energetic Matrix, a G.E.M., of which we are each an interconnected part. As interconnected energetic beings we are able to impact the Universe by our energy. In Chapter 2, we learned that we transmit an energetic pattern by our beliefs, emotions, thoughts and actions. This energy interacts with the Universe and the Universe, in turn, reflects back to us energy that is similar or complimentary to what we are transmitting. That reflected energy by the Universe can take the form of people, experiences and objects. Therefore, if we change our energy pattern in any way, the Universe must reconfigure itself in order to reflect back to us that which matches our new energetic pattern. This is the basis for the Third Law of Truth: Change anything and we change everything.

The smallest change creates a whole new reality.

We may believe that our world is a certain way and that there is nothing that we can do about it. We can believe that we are stuck with the way our life is going and what it has or does not have to offer us. There is, however, an alternative. We can simply change what we believe and adopt a new perspective. When we allow ourselves to change what we believe is true, even the by the smallest degree, at that very instant there is a shift in our energetic pattern. In that moment, a completely new reality is created within us and our world is a new place!

We have already created a new reality.

It may have sneaked up on us, but just by reading this we have made a change. Consciousness is that powerful and when we expand our consciousness, we in turn expand our reality. We are in a new place and everything is different.

Imagine standing outside on a clear and moonless night looking up at the stars. As we stand there, we look up and see the majesty and beauty of the heavens from our own unique perspective. Then, if we were to shift the position of where we were standing just slightly, we would be in a different place and all the stars would be in a different place relative to where we stood before. However small we may perceive our movement to be, it has resulted in changing how we perceive our world, our reality. We cannot see or experience the Universe the same from both places. Each position is unique and each offers a different perspective and experience.

As we learn, grow and expand our conscious understanding of our reality, we change it as well. The reality that we existed in and believed in before, the one that we saw as real and valid, no longer exists for us, because we have placed ourselves in a completely new one.

Conscious awareness connects us to a new reality.

Awareness alone is a powerful step towards change. Once we are aware of something, we are connecting to it. We are starting to steer a new course in our life. We are traveling in a new direction, to a new place in the Universe. In fact, a part of us, our consciousness–the part of us that transcends the physical dimension–has already arrived at the new destination! Time and space are not obstacles for our consciousness because that powerful portion of who we are can travel even faster than the speed of light. It can travel at the speed of consciousness. A change in consciousness changes us, changes our world and reaches into the farthest depths of the Universe.

Awareness changes us because we have expanded our consciousness to something new. Whether we believe in it or not, we have still allowed it into our consciousness and it is then subject to our willingness to accept it or reject it as Truth. It is through our consciousness that we are able to connect to all that the Universe contains: all the potential and possibility; all the reality and what we may believe to be "un-reality."

Reality is within our consciousness.

To understand just how powerful awareness alone can be, we must expand our notion of reality and where it resides. We often think of it as "out there somewhere" but really, where is it? Everything that we think of as being out there–people, experiences, and things– we must first bring within our consciousness in order to experience them. We experience that "outside" world by building our own version of it within us. All the experiences that we ever have, we have within our being. Therefore, where does reality really reside?

We may perceive it to be outside–but we can only experience it from within.

Our conscious experience of reality reaches beyond the physical. Yes, a portion of our life experience is made up of physical experiences in a world that we perceive to be physical. Yet, we are only really seeing and feeling a portion of the total reality of the Universe. In fact, our five senses are more like filters than open channels for all the energetic reality that exists. They work more in terms of limiting and restricting energetic information to specific wavelengths and frequency ranges, rather than to letting in all the information that is out there. Our five senses do help us experience life, but those sensory experiences are only a portion of what the Universe contains.

We experience physical and non-physical reality.

Our physical senses show us a part of the picture. Through conscious awareness, however, we are able to reach deeper into the Universe and experience much more of what it holds. In fact, a large portion of our lives is not a product of external physical sources but more a product of internal ones. We can experience emotions, ideas, thoughts, and see images in our minds that may seem to have no basis in reality, no outside physical representation or cause. We often experience things that are thought to be fantasy, "not real." For example, we can read a story in a book that we might call "fiction" or "not real." Yet we can still experience all kinds of very powerful things: fear, anger, jealousy, love and joy. Much of what makes us human can be created or stimulated within our being from so-called "non-reality." Is it real or is it not? The experience can seem very real. Even if we do not believe in the reality of the story, we can still be made to feel it. We can be engaged, activated and moved by words and images that can create for us a very "real" experience within our consciousness. It can be as "real" as any physical experience and sometimes even more profound. Likewise, we often have dreams so life- like that we wonder: "Am I awake, is this real?" We can also have fully awake conscious experiences and ask ourselves: "Am I dreaming?" The line between reality and so-called "non-reality" within our human conscious experience is often blurred and sometimes difficult to distinguish.

We cannot experience a non-reality.

The whole Universe is made up of energy in many different forms. As discussed before, some of it is measurable and some of it is not. Likewise, much of our human experience is also the product of many different forms of energy. We cannot, however, experience something that does not have energy to it. Experience on any level is some form of an energetic transformation and therefore some form of reality.

We have misled ourselves into believing in "non-reality," but really, it is just a product of classification. Yes, some things are physical and some things are not; some things have occurred and some have not yet come to pass; some things seem attainable and some things seem far-fetched. However, if we can hold any thought, feeling, or image in our consciousness in any way, in any form, then they have an energetic reality. This is a powerful concept and one that cannot be overlooked or discounted. Anything that we can hold in our consciousness is a real energetic reality!

Consciousness is a real place of real energetic power. What we do with that energetic power has real impact. Where that energy goes, how it takes form and what it does is very much a real phenomenon. Many take a large part of human conscious experience to be a place of fantasy or "non-reality;" a world set apart from the "real" world. What has really happened is that a line has been drawn, and a classification has been made to include "this" but not "that." Man divides and separates, classifies and segregates the world in effort to make sense of it. This may seem to be a useful strategy in some ways, but it can also become an obstacle in other ways, because the Universe is not a separated or divided amalgam. The Universe is a unified and interconnected energetic system. If we qualify, discount, or deny portions of what we may think of as "non-reality," then the potential of those aspects are put aside and their power is idled. However, if we value and claim all consciousness to be a real part of us and the Universe, then we are unlocking an unlimited place of power and potential within us.

We decide what is real.

We build our own version of the world that we believe is "out there" within our being. How we experience that world and ourselves is determined by our own conscious choice: deciding what is real and what is not, deciding what is Truth and what is falsehood.

Clearly, reality is not just what is physical–that which can be measured–because a great portion of our human experience is non-physical conscious experience. Reality is not only what can be experienced, because we know that we do not experience everything that is out there. Reality is not just what we know, because everyday, if not every moment, we expand reality by increasing our understanding and knowledge of it.

When we expand consciousness, we expand reality.

How we see the world is very important, because what we believe it to be, it is for us. The reality that we believe in, that we hold within our consciousness, can be very small or very large. Do not be misled into believing in only that which we have personally experienced or what others have experienced. Reality is much deeper, richer and expansive for those who consciously work towards making it so. We need to open ourselves up to more and more of what the Universe holds for us. When we choose to expand our reality, we are also expanding ourselves. We are part of the reality that we believe in. Expand one and we are expanding the other.

Change in consciousness restructures the Universe.

When we make a change on any level and in any way, that change reaches far beyond our physical reality. We are energetic beings and the major portion of our being is not bound by physicality, because it resides in a different dimension. Our ability to move and change in that dimension is unlimited and not bound by the constraints of this physical dimension. When we make a change in our consciousness, there is a shift on a much larger scale. We create a new version of ourselves and, because we are a new energetic pattern within the Universe, the Universe must then reconfigure itself and reform itself around us. There is a re-patterning and re-shaping of the energetic sea that the Universe is, so that what surrounds us matches who we have become.

Change is creating a new relationship with the Universe.

When we change how we relate to the Universe, the Universe, in turn, changes how it relates to us. This is a dynamic interaction between each one of us and the Universe. In that very moment, when we break through the shell of our old selves and expand out to include a new part of ourselves, we are a new creation. We are no longer the same person and the Universe is no longer the same Universe! We have not only changed who we are, we have changed the Universe. That is how powerful and far-reaching a change is in consciousness. That is how powerful and far-reaching we are. Think of a change in consciousness as an energetic wave that travels through us, out into the Universe, reverberating throughout, and then is reflected back to us. That reflected energy begins to change how we experience ourselves and how we experience the Universe. It does not happen tomorrow, next week, or sometime down the road, but right in that very moment.

We can feel the energy of Universe flow into us.

How many times have we thought of something new, a new or different possibility for ourselves or imagined ourselves doing something we had never thought of before? When that happens, we often feel something quite profound–a strong emotional response. What are we feeling? We are feeling the very energy of that potential or possibility for us. We have opened ourselves up to a new part of the Universe and it has already begun to flow into us. It is like opening a new door and a fresh, new, energetic breeze of possibility and potential begins to blow into our very being.

We often have very strong and physical responses to what we have been told are dreams or fantasy. However, we have been misinformed, because consciousness is real and anywhere and any place we go with it is also real.

Awareness is a connection to a real portion of the Universe.

If we can hold anything in our consciousness–if we can conceive of it, then it is a part of the Universe. Very importantly, it is also a part of us. When we connect to it with our consciousness, we are not connecting to something that is beyond us or outside of us. As we learned in Chapter 1, the whole Universe is a part of us and we are interconnected to it. When we expand our consciousness to something we perceive as new, we are not stepping outside ourselves, or stepping beyond our limits or capacity. We are just becoming aware of what we already contain.

Suppose that we lived in a very large mansion and, after living in it for many years, we believed we had a good understanding of what it was and what was in it. One day we are walking down a hallway in our mansion and we discover a door that we did not know was there. With excitement and a little trepidation, we open it up and look into a large and beautiful room full of all kinds of treasures, a room we had no idea was in our house. The room and all of its contents were in the house all along, but we were not aware of it. This is what happens when we expand our consciousness; we have the experience of becoming aware of part of the Universe that is also a part of ourselves.

In a very real way, our consciousness is able to travel and explore the Universe without limitation or boundaries.

Our notion of ourselves must change for us to become more fully aware who we truly are: energetic beings not bound or limited in potential but only beings that lack awareness and the willingness to believe in their greater Truth.

We choose to accept or reject portions of the Universe.

When we explore the Universe, we often come across new doorways. When we open our consciousness to them, the energy of those realities is able to flow into us and reverberate throughout our being. It is often in that very moment that we make a powerful choice, choosing to accept or reject the reality of something. In spite of our very real feelings, we will many times shut the door and walk away from that potential or possibility. We do that by not believing in that part of the Universe, denying the portion that contains that potential or possibility for us. This is where, so many times, we turn our back on ourselves and on the Universe.

We limit ourselves with disbelief.

Time and time again we limit ourselves, our world and even the Universe by our disbelief, saying in so many words: "That is not real, that is not possible and that is not true."

Just as our expansion can be dynamic, so too can be our contraction. When we deny the reality of something, in an instant our world is smaller place. The Universe, in response to our rejection, shuts down everything that was part of that reality, that potential and possibility for us. If we cancel our order, the Universe is not going to deliver the goods. It honors our choice. It is our free will to choose whether to accept or reject that portion of the Universe.

The Universe will not violate our sovereignty.

The Universe will not violate the sovereignty of our consciousness and force us to believe in something that we do not want to believe in. What we believe in is solely our choice. Our consciousness is our own dominion. This is truly who we are and this is truly our place of power. Yes, our body may fail us, or we may find ourselves imprisoned or bound by something that physically overpowers us, but our consciousness is a real place where no one can enter without our consent.

If we lock a door, it stays locked.

If we close a door, the door stays closed for as long as we choose: days, years, lifetimes and even eternity. However, the Universe will knock at the door from time to time. It will check in on us and see if we are interested in reconsidering. The Universe will try to get our attention and it will try to raise our awareness. Why is this so? This is because the Universe, as a whole, overall, is continually growing, expanding and changing in every moment. It is seeking to realize and demonstrate what is possible. The Universe is looking for those who are interested and willing to play a part in its expansion and growth. There are some who are choosing to play a part and some choosing not to participate. Some are even trying to make our world a smaller and more limited place. However, the energy, movement and momentum of growth and expansion of the Universe, in total, cannot help but rub up against us from time to time, regardless of our personal choice.

Awareness is the Universe asking us to decide.

Awareness is very important; it is not some kind of random occurrence in our lives. When we become aware of something, there is a reason for it. There is nothing in the Universe that does not have a purpose or reason or cause behind it. If something comes to our attention, if our awareness is raised to an aspect of our world, or to ourselves, it is asking for our conscious involvement. It is asking us to consider or reconsider it as a part of us, as a part of our life, as a part of the Universe. The Universe is getting our attention and giving us an opportunity to make a choice. It is asking us if we want to open the door or continue to keep it closed. Do we want to stay where we are or would we consider stepping forward into greater understanding?

Our beliefs are the gatekeepers.

We can open the door and look into a potential or possibility, but we can only step into that potential by believing in it. It is our belief in something that gives it the ability and permission to come into our lives. Our beliefs are the gatekeepers. We open and close the doors of the Universe by what we believe. Our beliefs decide what is possible and what will come true.

Awareness opens the door and allows us to consider a part of the Universe and feel its potential, but it is our conscious belief in it that allows us to fully step inside that reality. What we can hold in our consciousness is within our power, within our grasp and within our capability.

To change our lives we need to change our beliefs.

If we what to change our life, if we want to experience it differently, what can we do? We can simply change our beliefs. We can do a thorough housecleaning; casting out the beliefs that do not serve us and replacing them with ones that do. We must find all the beliefs within us that undermine or contradict what we want to be and where we want to go.

There are beliefs that can limit us.

Are our beliefs keeping us in one place or are they allowing us to expand, to grow, to move forward in life? When we begin to review our beliefs, look for words that limit us, stop us, that create fear, that divert us, that make us second-guess ourselves and our goals. There are multitudes of limiting beliefs, and our world is full of them. To get us started thinking about our own beliefs; let me list some common limiting ones:

"It's too hard."

"I can't do that."

"I don't know how."

"What good will it do?"

"I will never find someone."

"No one understands me."

"Nothing ever works out for me."

"It will never last."

"I'm too old."

"I'm too young."

"I'm not well enough."

"I'm not strong enough."

There are many beliefs that limit us and stop us from being the Truth of who we are. We can choose to believe in limitations, boundaries, and obstacles. We can accept them as reality, but there are people who have chosen differently. For every limiting belief that we may have, there are real life examples of people who have chosen to believe differently. There are people out there with situations much like our own, that have been able to push through limitations, overcome obstacles and reach their goals. What gave them the ability to do so? Their power came from believing that they could. Are they exceptional people? It all depends on what we think the rules are. For some the rule is: "Things work out and there is a way to reach our goals." This is how they approach life and the challenges that come their way. Why do we so many times believe that we are the exception to rule? Why do we believe that things work for others but not for ourselves? The Universe does not work that way. It works for you and me and for everyone, no exceptions. The rule is there are no exceptions.

We make up the rules that we live by.

We create the structure of our reality and that includes the rules. We decide what the rules are in life; the way we believe things work. Rules are powerful belief structures. They are templates that we live by. If we believe that life is difficult and hard, we create a world of difficulty and hardship.

Is it real? Yes. Everyone's reality is a real place. However, there is an infinite variety of different realities existing within the Universe and we have the ability to choose from any of them. To change our lives we must be willing to rewrite our rulebook. This can be one of the most difficult and challenging aspects of change, because we may have to scrap some rules or templates that we have used for a long time–maybe our whole lives–and build new ones. Not only must we change what we believe about ourselves, we must also change what we believe about other people, about the world, and about the Universe.

Change is a process of renewal on all levels.

When we make a change, we often underestimate its powerful effect. We are prone to thinking of things as isolated and not interconnected. However, change, which is an integral aspect of the Universe, is not an isolated or disconnected process. When we make a change in our consciousness, that change begins to affect everything on every level. We may begin to see things differently; we may begin to experience things differently. The people in our lives may begin to see us and react to us differently. This can be unnerving, can throw us off and even scare some. We may begin to experience changes in areas of our lives where we were not expecting changes. Those changes may be in our personality, they may be in our life style, and they may be in our preferences. We may be drawn to things that we had never had an interest in before. We may recognize some changes because they are significant and stand out against how we were before. Many times, though, change is subtle and not so apparent. Change is a process of renewal on all levels. Often we do not believe that we have changed, but the reality is that we do not recognize that we have. We often miss or overlook the many ways that the Universe has re-configured itself around us. We may continue to try to see things the way they were in the past and not how they actually are in the present. Many times, we try to interact with the world as we did in the past, but the new reality, the one that we created the moment we made a change, is waiting for us to see its Truth.

We may find that our work may no longer satisfy us. We may see our relationships begin to shift and change. Some relationships may ask for more intimacy, others may need more distance. We may begin to sense a new part of ourselves, discovering a new place within our being. In every part of our being and our lives, we must be willing to recognize that change is underway and allow it to reconfigure and reshape our lives. Because we have invited it in, we must also allow it to be what it is. Change is not holding on to the past nor is it closing the door to the future. It is making our reality work in a new way, so that we can be a new person. Change is creating a new relationship with the Universe.

We have the power to change ourselves, our experiences and our world, but we must focus very closely on what we believe. We must remove the beliefs that limit us and stop us and replace them with beliefs that free us to realize all the possibility and potential that we hold.

Strength comes from a solid belief structure.

To find the beliefs that would build the life that we desire, it is helpful to look at the beliefs of people that we would prefer to be like. If we wanted to build a house, we could learn from looking at other well-built houses. When we look at the differences in people, we see a wide range of personalities and life choices. We decide for ourselves the goals that we have in life and the type of person whom we want to be. There can be many versions of success and we must decide for ourselves what that is. There are many people in life that we might consider "successful" in some way. They might be very creative, have achieved a high level of education, developed a skill at something, or raised a family of very happy, well-adjusted children. What is it that makes these people able to achieve, where others often struggle and even fail at the same lifestyle or goal? When we look at the belief system of "successful" people, we often see a pattern. They have a cohesive belief structure, one that allows them to see themselves and the world in a way that is beneficial to them. They have strength of conviction, they believe in themselves, their abilities, and the goals they have for themselves and, therefore, they are able to persevere. Their beliefs are productive because they work together. Like a strong framework, each belief that they hold works to support their whole being and the goals they have chosen for themselves. Their whole belief system is carefully structured for accomplishing their goals.

We must carefully choose our beliefs.

Beliefs are so important that we want to be fully conscious of what we believe. Beliefs are not just statements, they are requests. When we believe in something, we are telling the Universe this is what we want; this is what we are choosing to accept into our reality. The Universe is full of all the potential that we can imagine and more, so we decide what to allow into our reality. The way we choose it, is by believing in it. When we believe in something, we are choosing it out of all the potential that is out there. We very selectively pick out the part of the Universe that we wish to experience.

Carefully choose our words.

Words are very powerful, and they must not be thought of as insignificant. There is no insignificance in the Universe and, therefore, every word that we use is very important. Words are energy forms. They are the building blocks that we use to construct our beliefs. Because of this, we need to pay close attention to the words that we use, as they will have a specific energetic effect. The Universe listens to us very closely and works to deliver to us exactly and precisely what we ask for. Listen to this statement: "I want to be a success." On the surface, this seems like an okay statement. However, wanting something is quite different than achieving something. If we tell the Universe that we desire to be in a state of wanting, it will bring us opportunities and support that allows us to experience a state of wanting. Often we hear people say "I will be a success." This is not altogether a negative statement. It is certainly more positive than "I will never be a success." It is definitely moving in a positive direction. Notice, though, that it implies that I am not a success yet. It is something that will happen in the future. It certainly gives us something to work for, but there is an even more powerful way to state what we desire: "I am a success." We are not putting the reality off into the future. We are stepping into it right now in the present. This is the most powerful way of communicating to the Universe what we believe.

I AM.

When we state to the Universe: "I Want," that statement creates the experience of wanting. When we state to the Universe: "I Will," that creates the experience of something happening in the future, but when we state: "I AM," this creates the experience of already being it in the present. The most powerful words we can say is "I AM." In this way, we claim ourselves, our power and all that the Universe holds for us. We can choose to say "I AM" a success, "I AM" abundant, "I AM" loving or whatever we choose to believe we are. When we state "I AM," we are opening ourselves up to the whole Universe and allowing all of it to be a part of us–everything that we can imagine and everything beyond our wildest dreams. When we state: "I AM," we are telling the Universe that we are claiming all of it to be a part of us. When we say: "I AM" we are telling the Universe what it already knows–we are the Universe! There are no boundaries, there are no barriers, and there are no limitations. In some way beyond our human comprehension, we are the Universe and the Universe is us. Where one begins and the other ends is really an arbitrary distinction. This is where our human consciousness is stretched to the breaking point, because for so many of us, we just cannot imagine how that can be.

For instance, the human body is perfect model of the Universe and this Truth. Our bodies are made up of billions and billions of cells. Each cell in our body has a particular job to do and each cell knows what that job is and how to do it. We have skin cells, bone cells, blood cells, brain cells and so on. To do the job and be the cell that each cell needs to be, each one has within it all the information it needs to do its particular job. What is quite remarkable is that, not only does each cell have all the information it needs to do its own job, it also holds within it all the information needed to create and maintain the entire human body. Why would that be necessary? We might think that a skin cell only needs to know about being a skin cell and not about being a blood cell, a bone cell or a brain cell. For some very important reason, all the cells are privy to all of the information. In spite of all the differentiation of shape, size and role that cells have within our bodies, they are able to work together to make the body the remarkable instrument that it is. Nature is a great teacher and it is telling us something very important here. Each cell needs to hold within in it a complete model, a diagram, a blueprint of the whole. Each cell contains the complete knowledge or consciousness of the body and the body in turn holds all of those cells within it. The interaction and communication of the entire knowledge with all the parts creates a unified cohesiveness. Each cell's knowledge or consciousness of the totality, plays a crucial role in enabling our bodies to exist and be the wonderful creations that they are.

Does a cell see itself as separate from the body because it is only outwardly expressing a part of the picture? Does the body see itself as made up of billions of cells expressing themselves individually in a particular way? Is there a need for one perspective over another; to see it one way or another? Likewise, do we really need to make a distinction between ourselves and the Universe?

Each one of us is a unique expression of the Universe. We are interconnected with the Universe in a very real way, and because of our interconnection, we have access to it and all that it contains. We have free will and we have the power to believe, feel, think and act as we choose. Even though our unique expression is only part of the totality of the Universe, our uniqueness does not separate us from the whole. The whole cannot be what it is without each one of us expressing ourselves uniquely.

We choose to believe in separation.

We are free to believe in separation if we choose, but if we believe we are separate, we are telling the Universe that is how we want to experience it. There are some of us who choose to believe that we are separate and there are those who want us to believe that. Yet, there really is no need for such a belief. By believing in separation, we create one type of experience. By believing that we are One with the Universe, we create another. We have, as a whole, largely been in the first camp for a very long time. We now have an opportunity, for those who are interested, to pull up stakes and move to a new camp, one that offers us so much more, individually and collectively. When we choose to say, "I AM," we are putting aside all that separates us from each other and from the Universe. We are saying: "We are the Universe".

The rate and degree of change is up to us.

If, and how, we make changes in our in life is our own personal choice. Some of us may choose to make dramatic changes and others may choose a more gradual approach. One way is not necessarily better than another, for we are each on our own unique journey. We must honor the way that we choose to reconfigure our lives.

Any change does change everything. How much of a change depends upon us. As we will see, our beliefs require us to place our trust in a particular reality. Some realities are slightly different and others are vastly different. Any change is significant but some changes have results that are more dramatic. We can change the course of our life just slightly, and in time, we will end up at a new destination. However, imagine if we choose to change our course dramatically.

Some beliefs have more power to affect our lives. One belief that we have discussed is believing that we can change. This belief unlocks our reality and gives us access to the Universe and all the potential it holds for us. The degree of change that we believe is possible and the power to make it a reality is a direct function of our level of trust. Trust is a very powerful part of our Truth. Let us explore it now.

IV.

The Fourth Law of Truth

OUR HOME IS WHERE WE PLACE OUR TRUST

WE ARE IN A VERY POWERFUL position and can take control of our lives in an incredibly strong way by becoming aware of our beliefs. We may have identified some beliefs that we desire to let go of and we may have become aware of some we wish to adopt. Many times this is where we struggle the most, making changes. We often feel uncomfortable and uncertain with the new, and may find it hard to step out and leave the comfort of the old.

New beliefs do create a new reality, a new experience in life. They are that powerful. When we adopt a new belief, we step beyond the doorway that awareness brought us to and into a different reality. We can feel the energy of this new place in the Universe as it flows into us. We often feel things we have never felt before, because we are in a place we have never been before. When we change our beliefs, we are quite literally changing our course in the Universe and are heading in a new direction. We may get scared because we begin to feel the movement in our lives. This is when we often retreat and attempt to step back into the old reality, but we cannot hold on to the old and expect to step into the new. This is the rub for many of us. We want to move forward, but we want to also hold on to the past. We cannot do both. We must choose. The power to make the choice lies solely with us. We can have one foot on the dock and one foot on the boat that will take us to a new destination, but there comes a point when the boat pulls away from the dock into the future and we will have to choose where we are going to stand: in the old or in the new.

Change requires trust.

Change requires us to use a very remarkable part of ourselves: our trust. Trust is often misunderstood, so we need to explore this to show us how we can use it fully in creating what we desire. Making changes is like climbing a ladder. We must let go of one rung in order to reach for the next, and we must lift our foot from the stability of the step that we are on to gain a foothold on the step above it. We could call this trusting in something that we have not yet really experienced, but remember that beliefs are merely thoughts that we hold to be true. Why not take a thought that we would prefer and place our trust in it? If we see a place that we would rather be standing, then step towards it. In order to do so, we have to let go of the old belief and find a footing in the new one.

We always use 100% trust.

Trust is such an important force in our lives and yet we so often misunderstand and misuse it. We say that we have too little or that some people have too much; that someone is being foolish to trust so freely. Children are so phenomenal at trusting in something. This is because they have often not had the experiences in life that have "taught them differently." We often misunderstand and misinterpret the outcomes in life. In the next chapter, The Fifth Law of Truth, I will show how our experiences in life are a reflection of the Universe supporting us in a perfect way.

Trust is a principle force in our lives, especially if we look at it as a form of energy. From that perspective, it is not that we do not trust, it is rather where we place our trust. In most cases, a young child is able to place 100% of their trust in something, like getting the lead role in a play at their school. Where as someone with more "experience" in life, perhaps an adult applying for a job, may only place a portion of their trust in their chances of getting a new job. For example, they may believe that they have a 50% chance of being hired and a 50% chance of not being picked for the position. The adult is still using 100% of their trust, but they are placing it in different places, different realities. The child, on the other hand, just bets "the whole house" on what they believe is possible. They place all of their trust energy in the belief that they will get the lead role. Will they get the role? Everything that we create in our lives comes to us as a result of our participation and that of the Universe. There are many factors involved here, but one factor that we have full control over is the portion of our energy that we place in believing that something is possible. The child has taken the very powerful energy of their trust and placed it completely in what they believe is possible. They have opened the door fully for that reality to come into their lives, whereas the adult has only opened the door partially. In the case of the adult, the Universe must work harder at pushing past their disbelief in order to bring them the reality that they say they desire.

Doubt is trust.

Doubt is also very powerful. It is said that doubt is a lack of trust. However, it is not an absence of trust, but trusting in a different outcome or different reality. Doubt is just as powerful as trust and just as able to create reality. Doubt has created many great manifestations. It has toppled great armies and stopped many potentially strong people in their tracks. When we doubt something, we are simply placing our trust in a reality that we believe in.

100% Trust=100% Power.

Trust and belief work hand–in–hand. If we understand that trust is energy, then we can see that a belief is only as strong as the degree of trust or energy we place in it. The more trust we have in a belief, the more powerful it becomes. One hundred percent trust equals one hundred percent power in our beliefs. We are all one hundred percent beings, each and every one of us. This is an important Truth. We are always whole beings, but many of us fractionalize our power and diminish our strength by how and where we place our energy. If we place our energy in trusting in negative or counter-productive beliefs, we are working against ourselves and we become a house divided against itself. Powerful people are able to place their power fully in what they believe, fully directing their energy into what they believe is possible, and therefore, increasing their ability to manifest the reality of what they want.

Our home is where we place our trust.

When we place our trust in something, we are actually literally placing ourselves into that reality. Our energy is not bound or limited to just the physical dimension, it is able to transcend it. When we believe in something, we are putting our energy, our consciousness, the most powerful part of our being, into the reality that we have chosen. Even if that reality has not yet even begun to materialize in our lives, we are able to, in a very real way, step into it by trusting in it, by believing that it is possible. We have the ability and choice of where to place our energy, and that energy is capable of reaching beyond the limits of time and space.

A dream is a potential waiting to be realized.

From childhood to adulthood, there are dreams that we have had–people, experiences or things that we have wanted to bring into our lives. The Universe is large and daunting, but we are not slaves to its wants and desires. In fact, we have been given a remarkable gift, which is free will. This ability to act independently and make choices allows us to participate in creating the life that we want for ourselves. In effect, our gift of free will has made us co-creators of our lives. We are participating in the process. However, there is frequently a gap between what we dream of and what we actually experience. To close that gap we need to look at what dreams are.

The Universe contains all potential and possibility.

When we think of dreams we think of something that is not yet real, something "out there" that we want to realize and bring into our reality. Dreams are potential forms of energy that exist in the Universe. The Universe contains all the potential of everything already: every idea, every thing, every experience and every being. In essence, nothing is really created because it already exists in the form of a potential or possibility.

Creation is a realization of potential within Universe.

When we say that we are creators, we are using the concept loosely. In reality, we manifest the potential of the Universe, bringing forth what it already holds within it. All that man has "created" came from the Universe and was realized because of a potential that already existed. Art, literature, music, and technology came from the non-physical and into the physical through humankind. We have the ability to real-ize, make real, energy that was in the infinite sea of possibilities and bring it into physical form. This is important because we all have, at our fingertips, an unlimited resource of unlimited potential: the Universe. The Universe contains all the potential that exists and will ever exist, the potential of the past, the present and the future. We are a part of it, it is a part of us and, because of that, we are able to tap into and access all that it contains.

We must connect with our dreams.

To realize or manifest something in the Universe, we need to make a connection to it, a connection between the non-physical dream and our physical reality. We can dream until the cows come home, but if we do not allow a way for our dreams to come to us, then our dreams cannot flow into our lives. To realize a dream, we must make an energetic pathway from one dimension to the other. If we do not believe in something, and do not trust that it is possible, then it will not happen. It cannot physically happen, because there is literally no way, no energetic avenue, in which it can travel to us. Everything is made of energy, including our dreams. All energy must flow along a conduit or pathway. In a sense, our belief is the pathway that allows a dream to come in to our life. Believing is an important part of manifesting our dreams into this reality.

Trust is taking a position of ownership.

When we place our trust in something, we are, in a very commanding way, taking ownership of it. We are literally buying into a part of the Universe, making it a conscious part of us. The more we trust in something, the more the dream (which is a part of the Universe) becomes part of us. We are no longer separated from each other by doubt or disbelief. When we choose to trust in something, we energetically redefine ourselves. The dream becomes us and we become the dream. Ownership is an important step in conscious understanding of the Universe. In previous chapters, we have been building on our understanding of the Universe. In The First Law of Truth, we learned that we are fundamentally interconnected with the Universe. In The Second Law of Truth, we learned that our beliefs open doorways to the Universe and all that it holds. In The Third Law of Truth, we learned that any change in consciousness changes our reality. Now, in The Fourth Law of Truth, we are learning that by placing our trust in something, we are "energetically" claiming ownership. We are staking a claim. It is very important that we understand how powerful this Truth is! If we own something then we have conscious power over it! When we own something, we do not think about whether we can use it, or whether we need some kind of permission to do so. Ownership gives us all the rights and privileges that are associated with having something: the control to influence it, to direct it and do what we choose to do with it. If we do not own it, (by not trusting in it), then it is outside us and beyond our control.

We can open ourselves up to our dreams.

When we believe in our dreams, we, in an "energetic" way, take ownership and close the gap between the non-physical and the physical Universe. Believing creates a conscious pathway in the Universe to our dreams. When we choose to believe in something we are simply saying to the Universe, "OK, I choose to believe in this," and the Universe in turn responds and opens the door to the potential of that dream. This is important! The pathway is our belief and our degree of trust controls how much of ourselves we place beyond the doorway and into the reality of our dream.

Trust opens the door to our dreams.

We can choose to open ourselves up to a small part of our dreams or we can choose to open ourselves up to all that they hold for us. It all depends on how much trust we are willing to invest in our dreams. It is up to how much of our energy we are willing to commit to that reality. We can decide and we have control.

Our degree of trust is the force that opens the doorway. Energy can, and does, flow both ways. Not only can we step into our dreams but also our trust allows them to flow into our lives. How much of our dreams are we willing to let into our lives? If we trust in our dreams just a little, the doorway to them is opened just a little. However, if we are willing to commit ourselves 100% by trusting 100%, then amazing things can and will happen in our lives!

The Universe responds to our level of commitment.

When we commit ourselves by trusting in a belief, we are using the energy of our consciousness in a very potent way. The Universe is always listening and responding to us. Not only does the Universe respond to our beliefs because of their specific energetic message, but the Universe also responds to the intensity of our beliefs. The degree of trust we place in our beliefs creates an energetic intensity. In turn, the Universe will match the energetic intensity of the transmission with supportive and complimenting energy in the form of people, experiences and things. If we only commit ourselves partially, the Universe is only going to respond to us partially. Our level of commitment is an important part of the energetic message that we send out to the Universe. How much of ourselves we commit to our dreams determines the degree of response by the Universe.

Belief + Trust=Reality.

Believing in something and then trusting that it can become a reality is crucial. Talk to anyone who has created something that did not exist in this dimension before. They were able to reach into the non-physical dimensions of the Universe and bring into physical reality that which they believed in and trusted was possible. The automobile, the airplane, the computer–all took root in someone's consciousness first. The people that created or contributed to these inventions did not wait to see them in order to believe in them. They were able to believe that it was possible and then trusted that it could be done. Creative and inventive people have this ability. They are able to stand on their beliefs and, with total trust, reach out, grasp their dreams, and pull them into reality.

Seeing is believing.

We have a common saying in our culture that "seeing is believing." Most people take this to mean that in order to believe in something, they must first be able to see it. The problem, though, is that most people are looking for reality in a limited place: they are looking in the physical dimension. They believe in something only when they are able to see it with their physical sight. The physical dimension is only a small fraction of the total Universe and those possibilities are already here; they already exist physically. To bring in something new, we have to look somewhere else. We have to expand our vision beyond the physical. There is a much more powerful, creative and unlimited place that we can all look in and it is not in the physical dimension. The place to look is in our imagination.

Our imagination is a real place.

We have learned that everything in the Universe is made of energy and that anything that we experience has an energetic component to it and therefore is real in someway. We have also expanded and even shifted our understanding of reality. Reality is not just what is out there, but that our consciousness is our reality. It is the only place we experience reality. For that reason, everything within our consciousness is real: a belief, a thought, a feeling, and even a vision. They are all real energy. Yes, the pictures in our minds are real things. If we can see it in our imagination, it is a real energy form and therefore exists on some level, in some way, at some time and in some place. Just because it is not physical, does not mean it is not real. The non-physical is very real and a very important part of the reality of the Universe as I have previously discussed. Therefore, if we can see it in our imagination, it is real and we can believe in it: "Seeing is Believing."

We can envision the potential of the Universe.

Creative and inventive people not only believe in something before it is a physical reality, but they are able to see it before others can. The power of imagination has been shown repeatedly to be very productive and useful to people involved in many different creative areas: inventors, playwrights, athletes, musicians, actors, and the list goes on and on. They actively use their imagination to visualize something that they want to create, or they use it to assist them in performing a task. The reason it works so well is that it is a real place, a real dimension. It is in this realm of non-physicality that creative people are able to see, that they are able to envision. People with vision are able to see into the higher dimensions of the Universe where all potential and possibility lives. Everything that can be seen, the entire physical Universe, comes from that place of infinite power and infinite possibility.

Our imagination is a powerful place

Our imagination is an energetic reality. It is how we access the higher, non-physical and infinite potential of the Universe and ourselves. When we go into our imagination, we are not just going into our own consciousness and ourselves, we are going into the non-physical and higher dimensions of the Universe itself. Why is it so powerful? It is powerful because there are no constraints, no boundaries, no limits and no time. It is where we are set free. Our imagination is the vehicle we can use to travel, explore and discover the unbelievable potential of the Universe and ourselves.

Our imagination is part of the non-physical Universe. It is the place where the unbelievable comes from, and where all the potential reality that will ever be already exists. This is where we will find our roots, because this is where we are from. This boundless and unlimited portion of the Universe is where the greater portion of our beings resides. Why not use the most powerful parts of ourselves? It makes sense to do so. We need to treat our imagination with respect, develop it, use it, and most importantly, put our trust in it. It has a lot to tell us about ourselves and about the Universe. We open ourselves up to the Universe by what we believe and trust in, not just conceptually or philosophically but on a real energetic dimension. Our beliefs are real pathways in the Universe: our trust is a real energetic force that allows us to unleash the enormous power and potential that is waiting to be expressed through us.

When we trust in a future we believe in, that future can become a reality because we have, in fact, already stepped into it and made it our home.

V.

THE FIFTH LAW OF TRUTH

THE UNIVERSE SUPPORTS OUR
TRUTH IN A PERFECT WAY

AS WE HAVE BECOME more aware of our power and position in the Universe, we can see that what we generate energetically has incredible impact on our lives and the lives of others. What we experience in life is not random phenomenon, but a result of our energetic power interacting with the energetic Universe. How the Universe responds to our energy is not a random or haphazard process, but a precise one. The Universe responds to or supports our energy, our Truth, in a way that is perfect.

To understand this perfect support, imagine that the Universe is a grand computer that reads our total energetic output and then calculates an exact energetic response to it. The Universe then sends that energetic response back to us in the form of people, experiences and things, which then flow into our lives. The more conscious and aware we are of what we believe, the more likely we will understand the Universe's support. However, there are people, experiences, and things that show up in our lives that do not seem to fit or make sense. We often see them as faults, glitches or anomalies of some kind. We can be confused and thrown off by this. The Universe, though, is always working to give us precisely what serves us the best. It is not working against us; but working with us and for us. Everything in our lives is a reflection of who we are, our Truth. If we misunderstand the people, experiences and things in our lives, then we are misunderstanding ourselves.

The Universe reflects our conscious and unconscious aspects.

We have talked about how our beliefs are some of the most powerful conscious ways that we can communicate with the Universe. To understand our lives and that which does not seem to fit, we must be aware that we are also communicating with the Universe in unconscious ways. The Universe is always showing us the Truth of who we are. The experiences in our lives that do not make sense, are reflections by the Universe of the parts of ourselves that we are not conscious of, parts of ourselves we do not know we contain.

We are not yet conscious of our totality.

As we will see, a large and very important part of our purpose here on earth is to grow and develop our consciousness. We are here to learn about ourselves, as well as the Universe. We are vast and complex beings that have only gained a fraction of the understanding of our capability and ourselves. It is important that we become aware that we are on a journey of exploration, and that it is yet to be completed. We have not charted or mapped the totality of who we are and, therefore, we must be open to–and allow for–the unknown. We must be open to the aspects of ourselves and our experiences in life that are yet to be understood.

Our unconsciousness also interacts with the Universe.

We have not gained full consciousness of our totality. In the First Law of Truth, I talked about how we are multi-energetic and multi-dimensional beings and that we are made up of energy that is physical and non-physical. There are aspects of our energy that can be measured and quantified and there are aspects that cannot. The parts of ourselves that we are not aware of are, for now, the unconscious or unknown energetic aspects of our beings.

Who we are as individuals is a unique matrix of energetic patterns. Not only do our energy patterns contain all that we are aware of regarding ourselves (our beliefs, experiences, knowledge and so on), but we also contain the energy of those aspects or parts of ourselves that we are not yet aware we contain. Regardless of our conscious awareness, those unconscious aspects are interacting with the Universe and the Universe is responding to them.

The Universe is fully conscious of our totality.

The Universe is fully conscious and energetically knows the totality of who we are and all that we contain. Even though we may only be conscious of a portion of our being, the Universe is conscious, aware and interacting with the totality of each one of us.

The Universe is perfect.

The Universe is perfect because it is complete. There are no missing parts or elements within it. The Universe is changing within every moment of time and every moment outside of time. However, all that is going on within it never changes its perfection. Change is not a process of getting better or getting worse. Change is a process of transformation. The Universe is one energetic sea in a continual process of change.

Therefore, if the Universe is perfect, then everything that makes it up is also part of the perfection. Not only are the elements that are part of its structure perfect, but the events and movements of all of its elements are perfect. How the Universe responds to us, the people, the experiences, the things that show up in our lives are exactly and precisely part of that perfection.

The Universe has a precise and very exact way of working. It is not careless or haphazard. There are no defects or flaws in the structure of the Universe and there are no defects or flaws in us or in our lives. Our lives are exactly what they need to be at this moment.

We are perfect.

Each one of us is a perfect creation. We are not defective, damaged or flawed in any way. There is nothing in the Universe that is a mistake and everything that comes from it is perfect. Every single part, aspect and creation of the Universe has a reason and serves a purpose. Each one of us, at this very moment, is a unique and perfect expression of the Universe. In the next moment, we may choose to be different and we would be just as perfect. Like the Universe itself, our lives are constantly in a process of change. Is a child more perfect when it is born than when it is a day, a week or a year old? Each moment is unique, completely different and perfect.

We get confused about this. We look around and see differences in ourselves and in others; we see a world full of different choices and expressions and we make judgments about those differences. We think that some things are better and some things are worse. We believe that some things fit and some things do not. However, these are the judgments of humankind and not judgments of the Universe. Nothing that you or I may believe, feel, think, or do can diminish our individual expressions of perfection.

We talked about differentiation in the First Law of Truth. We learned that differences are the very structure and strength of the Universe. Judgment comes from not being aware that something, although different, still serves a purpose, plays a role and is perfect. It is from ignorance, not knowingness, which we judge. If we were fully conscious of the purpose and the role of something, we would not judge it because we would know how perfectly it fits into the grand design of the Universe.

The Universe values everything.

The Universe is fully conscious and, therefore, knows the cause and purpose of everything. It does not judge something as having more or less value. The Universe knows and values everything within it. The Universe knows the cause and purpose of everything that it contains and is quite able and capable of placing each piece, each part precisely where it fits and needs to be. Not only is the Universe doing this on the grand scale of universal creation, it is also creating a perfect experience for each one of us. This is what the Universe is doing in the puzzle of our lives. It is very carefully placing the pieces exactly where they go.

Humankind judges largely from ignorance.

When we make a judgment, we are saying that something has more value than something else does or that something is right and another is wrong. Judgment is taking a position on something that is supported by "knowledge" of the situation. Like a judge in court, we must gather the available information or facts, weigh the evidence and then come to a judicial decision. However, the decision that comes from our judgment is a relative Truth or understanding. Most often, we are working with limited information. We do not always have all the facts. To be able to reach "The Truth," we would have to be fully aware of the totality of the Universe and everything within it. We would have to have full and complete conscious understanding of how everything works, how every part fits, and have total comprehension of all the workings of the Universe. I would venture to say that human consciousness is not there, at least for now. Therefore, when we judge something we are doing so from a limited position and a place of ignorance about the larger picture. We are shooting in the dark, operating with limited knowledge, and as a result, very much open to error. The symbol of justice that we often see–with the blindfolded woman holding the balance of justice–is quite revealing. When we put on the robes of a judge, we are also putting on the blindfold.

Judgment creates separation.

When we judge, we are creating a division or separation in our reality. Division and separation are a construct, an artificial scheme because the Universe is not separated or divided. When we tell the

Universe that this is how we believe things are, we are really telling the Universe how to work. Even though the Universe knows the Truth, it will listen to us and try to work the way we say it must. The Universe will then create for us the experience of separation and division. When we judge, we separate ourselves from parts of the Universe. In essence, we disassemble it and put it back together the way we believe it should be constructed. It is like taking a car apart and then, in the process of putting it back together, we may throw away the pieces that do not seem to fit, we do not like or do not think are necessary. The problem is that those pieces are serving a purpose; they have a role in making the car function properly. With those pieces removed or put where we believe they should go, the car would not operate as it was designed-it may not be able to move, steer, stop, or protect us in a crash.

When we judge ourselves, or others or aspects of our world, we are telling the Universe what is of value and what is not. Our judgment breaks down the finely tuned and complex workings of the Universe and we, in many ways, blindly put it back together our way. In essence, we are telling the Universe how it should be and how it should work.

It would make sense that if we are not yet conscious of all the workings of the Universe and the role of every part and its proper position, we would be wise to make a choice to trust it, allow it to be and work the way that it does. We need to step into a new understanding of the Universe and ourselves. We need to put aside our judgment of ourselves, of others and our world, and begin to value and trust the totality of the Universe.

Preference is the power we have to choose.

There is a way we can select from what the Universe holds without making a judgment. We can have a preference. Preference is the power to choose. Preference is not a judgment, but rather the gift of free will that allows each of us to make our own choices. For example, rather than saying that we hate blue, red is ugly, and green is a much better color, we can say that we prefer green. There is no judgment involved in stating a preference. The Universe allows us the opportunity to choose what we desire without judging. We do not need to separate and degrade those aspects of the Universe that are not our preference. This may seem a subtle difference to some, but it is not. When we prefer something, we are allowing those aspects of the Universe that we do not prefer to be a part of the whole, and importantly, a part of us. Even though we may not prefer some aspects, they may play a part or a role in allowing us to experience our preferences. We may not like the colors red or blue, but together they create the color green. Without them, we could not experience the color that we prefer. Preference is enabling us to direct our lives and still allow the Universe to work in a way that is in alignment with its perfect structure and design.

We are perfect and our lives are perfect. Our lives are just what they need to be in the moment. However, they can change. We can, if we decide, create a different and perfect version of ourselves. We can create a different and perfect life experience. We can create a different and perfect world. Because we have free will, we have the ability to choose. We have the ability to choose how we experience life. The Universe is full of an infinite number of different possibilities and we can each make our own choices. We have been granted the power to exercise our free will to have a preference.

Our power comes from our ability to choose.

The power we have as individuals is our ability to choose, to make a choice. Without this, we are powerless. When we believe we cannot choose or we have no choices to make then we are held captive. There is nothing that can be done for us or by us to set us free.

Many things—both mental and physical—can enslave us. However, even if we were the weakest person with the smallest degree of consciousness, we would still have the ability to make a choice. Within us, there is place, a definitive and decisive part of our being, where we can exercise this power. That conscious power to choose is what makes us who we are. How we use, or do not use, that part of ourselves, creates us. It makes us the individuals that we are and it creates our reality. We are our choices.

We have often disregarded the power and impact of our choices and have placed the responsibility for our choices outside of ourselves. When we do this, we disconnect ourselves from the very source of our personal power.

This act is what enslaves us. We bind up our free will. Freedom is not something that we earn; it is something that we give away. We make the choice to believe that we have no choices. We make the choice to believe that others are better at choosing for us and we often choose to believe that the Universe is choosing for us without our consent. Free will is the essence of what makes us human. We so often fail to realize that our free will is our fundamental source of individual power and the fundamental creative force of the Universe itself.

When the infinite potential of the Universe is combined with the creative power of free will, there is an explosion of boundless possibility.

All creation comes from this synthesis. The Universe is one energetic sea manifesting an infinite range of different choices.

Our ability to choose is the very source of Universal creative power that we all hold within us. If we give away our free will to choose, we give away our soul. When we embrace our free will–when we believe that we can always make a choice–we claim ourselves, the creative essence of the Universe within us and we step into the seat of our power.

There are no right or wrong choices.

What should we choose to be and which direction should we go? There are no "right" or "wrong" answers. It all depends on what we want to experience and it all depends on what we want to create or manifest in our lives and the lives of others. The Universe is an infinite place of infinite possible choices. The Universe is not telling us what to be or what to do or which way to go. Our choices are ours to make. The Universe does not give us free will and then turn around and take it back. It is not choosing for us. The Universe has granted us freedom and privilege to choose for ourselves.

Power and responsibility come together.

Many do not want to take the responsibility or the accountability for their lives and their choices. However, we cannot have power and not be responsible for it. Power and responsibility are bound together. We are accountable for what we create, consciously or not. The Universe holds us accountable only because our choices have consequences. These consequences are built into the structure of the Universe. Every choice comes with its own set of possible experiences and possible outcomes.

If we choose to ride a bicycle and we lose our balance and fall, is the bicycle at fault? Is the road or gravity to blame? The choice to ride a bicycle has its own set of potential experiences. When we choose to ride off on our bicycle, we are signing up for–and opening ourselves up to–all the potential experiences that may result. Is the Universe punishing us when we fall? No, but falling is a possible outcome or consequence of our choice.

Is the Universe heartless and uncaring for not protecting us from life's pains and hardships? Many times, it may seem so from man's point of view. However, the Universe is fair and just. It does not apply the rules to some and exclude others. The Universe is not biased or prejudice. The rules apply to all and all are held accountable to them. All the forces that come to bear on us when we ride a bicycle are the same for all of us: gravity, inertia, momentum and so on. However, it is our own individual uniqueness and ability to choose that make our choices an infinite well of possibilities and potentials. Where one person may fall and never get on a bicycle again, someone else may not let the painful experience stop them from getting back on the bicycle. That person will know even more fully the reality of potentially falling. The person who chooses to continue to ride may go on to challenge themselves and their abilities. They may learn and develop the ability to climb hills, as well as the nerve and skill to speed down from their summits. Is riding a bicycle all fun? Many times a lot of effort and determination is required. We can choose to ride around the block or we can choose to ride around the world.

Life is full of all kinds of experiences. Some are joyful and some are painful, some are challenging and some are effortless. Is the pain and effort worth the joy and the exhilaration that we may or may not experience? That is up to each one of us. However, do we stop living our lives when we fall? Does the pain (in whatever form) keep us from engaging in life or moving forward? Some people do choose to stop moving forward. Some people even choose to disengage from life. There are people that get on the bike and ride through life without ever falling and there are some that fall all the time.

Is that fair and just? It often does not seem so. Why do some suffer so much and others very little at all? This has been a subject of much discussion for millenniums. Humankind has taken many different positions on this. Are our life experiences dictated or chosen, or just good or bad luck?

What we experience in life is the product of many factors. Some things that happen seem to be dictated by forces that appear to be outside us. Our lives are subjected to many forces in the Universe that we can identify: the forces of nature, genetics, heredity and environment. The forces of humankind also influence us: family, culture, and government. There is, however, a large portion of our life experiences that are clearly a result of our own conscious and not–so–conscious choices. We could then say that our lives are a product of what we are choosing and a product of what we may say is outside of our control, such as acts of nature and acts of humankind.

We can choose to take responsibility for our choices. However, we often struggle in this area. We are good at taking responsibility when things go our way, but we place blame elsewhere when things go "wrong." As we grow and mature, we become more aware of the responsibility that we have in life and how life does holds us accountable for the choices that we make. However, where do we place the responsibility for all the things we experience that we do not understand, the events that seem to come to us from somewhere else? Where does the responsibility then lie—with us or with the Universe?

Taking responsibility is claiming our power!

We must make a choice. Either we are in the driver's seat or we are not. Some people believe that they have no control over their lives. Others believe that they have some control, but not about everything. They believe that there are certain things that are beyond their power and influence. However, what if we believed we had power over it all? The responsibility for our lives would then be solely in our hands. Some may see this as a tremendous burden and a frightening choice to make. In reality, it is a tremendous opportunity. In order to claim 100% of our power, we must then also assume 100% of the responsibility for what we create. Remember that everything is energy. Our power is energy. There is an equation that clearly expresses this:

100% responsibility = 100% power

What percentage are we willing to claim for ourselves? We might claim 20% responsibility for our lives and give the rest away. Many people do just that, they turn the responsibility for their lives over to someone or something else. However, if we want to have 100% of our power we must also assume 100% of the responsibility for it. When we choose to accept 100% responsibility, we place ourselves squarely in the driver's seat. Does this position make us more powerful or greater than we should be?

The Universe does not draw a line in the sand and say, "Don't step over this, you can only be this much and not any more." The Universe does not draw lines separating you, me, or anyone from all that it is. Only humankind creates separation and division. The Universe allows us to have 100% of our power if we are willing to choose to take 100% responsibility for it.

We have chosen this life for ourselves.

If we have the power to choose and the Universe does not choose for us, then being in this physical dimension at this time must have been our choice on some level. Conscious of it or not, all of us have chosen to be here. This physical dimension is a remarkable place and a remarkable choice. Choosing this took enormous courage and strength on our part because this place is not for the weak of heart or the timid of spirit. Being here says something about who we are, because this is a place that offers unique, powerful and intense experiences that cannot be experienced anywhere else in the Universe.

It took strength to come here because we had to accept the physical limitations and boundaries that are a part of this experience. In choosing to come here, we had to accept a physical body that can have varying degrees of abilities and inabilities. We cannot have a physical experience without a physical body. We may see our body as a burden and a hardship, but it has allowed us to experience this unique place of enormous potential and possibility.

Imagine a powerful being, one with incredible strength, making a choice to take on a condition that would make them weak. It takes strength for the powerful to choose weakness, as much strength as it takes those that believe they are weak–to choose power.

Imagine a boundless being, one with incredible courage, making a choice to take on a condition bound by limitation. It takes courage for the boundless to choose limitation, as much courage as it takes those that believe they are limited–to choose to be unbound.

This is a dimension rich with experiences.

Our experience in this dimension is full of diverse ranges of physical experiences: pain and pleasure, joy and sadness, health and illness, birth and death. From the moment of our birth, we are plunged into a world that is both painful and joyful. A child is quite upset by the new world outside the womb and is shocked to take that first breath on its own, when it feels the cold air rush into its lungs for the first time. In time, the child adjusts and becomes accustomed to its new environment, finding comfort and nourishment from its mother. For the mother, the pain of labor can be tremendous, but the joy of seeing her child, of holding it in her arms, of feeling its warm body against her own, can overshadow the pain, transform it, and help her accept the pain as a part of the human experience. To be human and to have the full human experience, we must accept life in all fullness.

To choose to have a child and then say, "I don't want it to be painful," "I don't want to have my feelings hurt," "I don't want to be sad when my child falls and scrapes their knee," is not having the full experience of being a mother or a father. It is the whole experience of life, which makes it so fulfilling. Pain and sadness make pleasure and joy the experiences that they are as much as pleasure and joy make pain and sadness the experiences that they are. They all work together to create the human experience. If we say we only want a part of the experience, then we are not stepping fully into this reality and we end up living a partial life.

Reward without effort is barren; effort without reward is fruitless.

If we are not open to all that life holds for us, then we are asking the Universe to create for us a partial experience. If we tell the Universe that we only want the pleasure of being a parent and not the pain, we are putting limits on our experience. In an effort to shield ourselves from some aspects of life we can end up empty handed and empty hearted.

To accept the fullness of the Universe, we must accept all that it contains. To accept the fullness of life in this physical dimension we must accept that everything in it is serving a purpose for us.

Taking responsibility is conscious power.

If we choose to take responsibility for our lives and everything in them, we are stepping into a completely new and very powerful level of consciousness. Taking responsibility is not putting the power and role of the Universe aside and doing things for ourselves. Taking responsibility is conscious recognition of our relationship with the Universe. It is a conscious understanding that we co-create reality with the Universe. If we believe that we are creating our lives by ourselves, we are not recognizing the power of the Universe. Likewise, if we believe that the Universe is creating our lives for us, we are not recognizing the power of our choices.

The Universe supports us unconditionally 100%.

The Universe lets us choose and then does everything it can to help us realize that choice. It does not matter what that choice is. The Universe does not give us 100% support for some choices and then hold back for others. The Universe does not have its own agenda for us. It is not trying to steer us in a particular direction of its choosing or lead us along in life because it thinks we should do this and not that.

An analogy of this is the unconditional support a parent could give to their child. Imagine a child that loves to paint and one day tells their parent that they want to become a famous artist when they grow up. A parent that honors the child's belief in their potential would do everything in their power to support the child in any way that they could to make that a reality for their child. They might surround the child with all kind of paints, canvases and brushes. They could enroll them in classes and take them to galleries and museums so their child could have everything possible in their lives to support their choice to be an artist. A parent that unconditionally supports their child would be willing to work two jobs or borrow money, if necessary, to create these experiences and opportunities for their child. Such a parent values and supports their child's belief and respects the choice the child has made and is committed 100% to supporting them in every way that they can.

The Universe is no less committed to us and does everything it can to support us 100% unconditionally in whatever we choose. The Universe is willing to do this because it values and honors our choices. The Universe respects any choice that we make, even if those choices limit us or steer us from our potential. It may seem like the Universe has turned its back on us at times, but all it has ever done, or will do in the future, is support what we choose. Any other action would be a violation of our free will. The Universe does not break its agreements. Therefore, it is bound to support only what our belief system allows, nothing less and nothing more. If we believe we are powerless, the Universe is going to provide us with opportunities to experience powerlessness. If we believe we are empowered, the Universe is going to provide us with opportunities to experience our empowerment. Whatever our Truth is, it is energetically directing the Universe to support that Truth in our lives 100%.

Everything in our life is the Universe supporting us.

There are people, experiences and things that may show up in our lives that we do not understand or that do not make sense to us. We may disregard these aspects of our lives as not applying to us. However, there are no extraneous or pointless events in the Universe or in our lives. Everything that we experience has something to do with us on some level. Our life, and everything in them, is the Universe supporting us perfectly. Our lives would be entirely different if they were not serving a purpose for us just the way they are right now.

Our lives are the solution to our problems.

The Universe is always there for us, supporting us 100% in being the person we believe we are in a world that we believe is real. If we choose to believe this, then everything that shows up in our lives is part of that support. Everything! Even the "problems" that we may perceive to have in our lives are not really "problems"–they are solutions. The Universe is trying to communicate with us through those "problems." The Universe is trying to tell us something important. It is always reflecting back to us the answer to the energetic equation of our being. The people, experiences and things that are in our lives are there precisely for us to gain a greater understanding of just who we are and what we believe in. Everything in our lives is there for the purpose of finding the answer to a much larger question: what is our Truth?

Imagine that you are sailing a boat on a journey across the ocean. You are a competent captain because you have had much experience at sea, encountered many difficult situations over the years and have developed a solid sense of seamanship. Your journey, although difficult, is still within your comfort zone. During your voyage, a storm comes up. You have been in many storms before and you know what to do. You set your sails, secure the hatches and gear in order to minimize the risk to you and your boat. At first, you feel like things are under control. However, the storm continues to intensify and reaches a level that you have never encountered before. It takes all your strength just to hang on, let alone try to maintain your course. You feel the storm is challenging you, testing you in every way that it can. You are afraid and you really start to think about your life, because you begin to feel the very real possibility of losing it. The unexpected storm that has crossed your path is speaking to you on a very deep level. It is bringing out, from the depths of your being, great emotion. You have never felt so alive and at the same time so afraid. You see yourself and your life, as you never have before, because there is such clarity in the moment that it astounds you. You feel the very power of the Universe bearing down on you. In this defining moment of your life, you are being asked to make a choice. The instant you choose life, a powerful force begins to rise up within you to meet the challenge head on. You gain a level of strength and courage that seems to be coming from somewhere beyond you and within you. In that moment, you feel the very Truth of your being and you will never be the same again.

Life is a journey of growth.

The unexpected, mysterious and challenging aspects of our lives are serving an important purpose for us. They are providing us with opportunities for growth: growth in awareness, growth in experience and growth in consciousness.

They can make us encounter parts of ourselves that we are unaware we contain. We may think that some of the things that happen to us in life are blowing us off course. However, it is what we experience in life and how we choose to experience it that allows us to travel within ourselves, taking a journey that brings us to the real destination—a new level of conscious understanding of our Truth.

The Universe as a whole is growing. It is moving towards the realization of its boundless potential. We are free to go along with the movement and direction of the Universe or not. It is up to us. We can stay where we are or we can, if we choose, journey towards the realization of our own unique potential.

An analogy is to imagine a large river coursing along on its way to the ocean. As the volume and current of water finds a way to its destination, there are many variations in its path. These variations are caused by changes in the topography of the landscape; a river's journey is often characterized as an ebb and flow. The river flows fast and furious through the narrow canyons of the mountains and then meanders wide and slow through the large valleys and flat plains. Along the river's course—here and there, from time to time—are pockets of water that form just to the side of the main flow of the current. These are called eddies. Water that was once heading for the boundless ocean is caught, whirling and swirling off to the side of the main flow of the river. In spite of all the power and force of the mainstream moving towards its destination, the water within the eddy remains captive.

Growth is a choice.

It is our choice whether to move forward or not. We chose to come to this remarkable place and we now choose how to use the opportunities and the potential that this experience can offer us. Growth is a choice. We can be like a student that signs up for a class, pays the tuition, comes to class and then doesn't listen to the lectures presented by the professor, doesn't read the books or materials or participate in the group projects. Choosing to take the class can be many things to many people. We are remarkable beings because of our free will and there are wide ranges of choices. There are also wide ranges of levels of participation in life. Even though we may come to class, we may decide to daydream or take a nap. We can participate very little or we can choose to get the most we can from our opportunity to learn and grow.

Our life is our choice and our responsibility.

It is up to us to choose what to believe about our purpose, why we are here and where we want to go! That is our choice and our responsibility. Our choices in the past have brought us to where we are today. Right now, though, we are at a very powerful position in consciousness, we are at a crossroads. At the very least, we are aware that the choices we make now and in the future can have the ability to unleash the power and potential of the Universe to make those choices a reality for us. It is up to each one of us to choose for ourselves: are we willing to believe we have this power? Are we willing to put our trust in that belief? What we have believed in the past has created our lives in the past and brought us to this point in consciousness and to this place in the Universe. What are we willing to believe about our lives? Where would we like to place ourselves in the Universe?

My life is an accident.

My life has a purpose.

My life is meaningless.

My life is meaningful.

My life is about working hard and gaining favor.

My life is about having pleasure and avoiding pain.

My life is about survival.

My life is about giving.

My life is about taking.

My life is about experiencing.

My life is about loving.

My life is about growing.

Whatever decision we make will set in motion the Universe's power to support that particular reality in our lives. Not having an idea about it, or believing that we do not have to make a decision, is still making a choice. The course and direction of our lives is not something the Universe has chosen for us. Even though, as a whole, the Universe is expanding and moving towards the realization of its own collective potential, it is our decision to participate in that or not.

We have chosen a destination in the Universe.

The moment we decided on anything at any level of consciousness, the Universe started to move us in the direction of that reality. The Universe did not choose the course our lives are taking at this moment. We did. We have set a course and we are underway towards the realization of a potential that we believe is true and real. Whatever we decided our lives were about, that choice created a destination in the Universe. We are creating a present and potential reality, whatever it is, moment to moment. In spite of what we may believe, feel, think or act out in our lives, we are at the controls and we are coursing towards a potential that we have chosen.

We have chosen growth.

We may or may not be conscious of a powerful Truth: we have chosen growth. We came here looking for opportunities to grow and expand our consciousness. If we had not made this choice, we would not be here on earth and we would not be reading this book about growth in consciousness. There are beings that will never come to this place in the Universe because it does not support them and the choices they have made.

We have chosen growth because there is a part of ourselves that we are looking for, a portion that we can feel exits. We may perceive it to be out there somewhere. However, it is actually within us, calling for recognition and drawing us towards itself. There is a powerful drive inside of us to claim what is rightfully ours; we are searching for our greater Truth. We are on a journey home to a place, to a reality, that words cannot begin to encompass nor quantify its magnitude. That drive within us to find our greater Truth has placed us on this path and given us the courage to choose to come and have this life experience.

The natural course of life is evolution.

Choosing to grow and change is a powerful choice; it is same choice the Universe as a whole has made. Here on earth, we can see how this path has led to an amazing realization of potential. All the diversity of life on earth is the result of a process called evolution. Evolution is a creative way in which life, over time, is able to adapt to changes in the environment. It is a process where nature is able to select or choose specific changes and carry these changes forward to the next generation. Evolution is not just any change; it is change that is productive and beneficial. It is change that allows life to flow in a new and more successful way. A successful change in the genetic blueprint is then passed on to the next generation. Darwin defined this success as "survival of the fittest." This is often misunderstood to mean physical strength. Darwin was talking strength, but a strength that had many more dimensions to it.

When we think of "survival of the fittest," we tend to think of the strongest male fighting to win the right to pass on his genetic template and preventing the "less fit" males from doing so. "Fittest," however, is more than brute force or physical strength. Where is the benefit if the strongest male mates with a female that is not a strong mother, one that is not able to carry, bear, then nurture, and protect her offspring? What good is it if the offspring are not raised in a strong environment that teaches them how to survive and how to parent? We see this demonstrated quite dramatically in our zoos these days. We are seeing rare and endangered animals that appear to be strong and powerful, unable to procreate or care for their offspring. In nature, they would be selected out as "unfit," their "weakness" would make them unsuccessful. Being "fit" means strength in nurturing, protecting, teaching, learning and more.

In nature, growth is beneficial if it makes life more successful in some way. Natural selection is a process that allows beneficial changes, changes that "strengthen" life to be passed forward to the next generation. It is a clear and decisive tool of nature that supports the evolution and realization of the magnificent display of life that we see on this planet.

Consciousness is evolving.

We are here to play a larger role than just the biological development of our species on this planet. Not only is there an evolutionary process taking place within the many forms of life on earth, there is also an evolution of something else. The Universe has created a reality, an environment that supports a tremendous opportunity for growth and development of physical life, as well as something even greater. It is through this unique and remarkable experience that we can choose to develop and advance the most amazing part of our being, our consciousness.

The life we are living is an avenue for us to discover who we are. There is no other place in the Universe where we should be, other than right here and right now. The Universe has made an incredible investment in us in creating this tremendous opportunity. This is a very important point in our development. We have not only chosen to grow, but we have also carefully chosen to have this particular life, at this particular time, and in this particular place to facilitate our progress.

Within each of our own personal lives, there is a treasure rich with possibility and potential. We may choose to find, open and discover what is inside. We are not random creations and we are not having a random or chance experience here on earth. The Universe, with our help and direction, is creating this very specific, individual and perfect experience to give each one of us an opportunity to discover our Truth.

VI.
DISCOVERING OUR
GREATER TRUTH

IN SPITE OF ALL OUR EFFORTS, and in the face of all the support, strength and power of the Universe, we can still get stuck in life. The barriers and obstacles that can stop us from advancing and developing our potential are not made of stone or steel. Our progress can be brought to a halt by something much stronger and more powerful. It is something within our consciousness. It can be one belief or it can be many. If we are at a standstill, then somewhere along the way we took on a belief that is thwarting our growth. We have lost our way by believing in something that has stopped us cold.

Our growth can be blocked by what we believe.

Our growth in consciousness can stall for many reasons. Many times, we have made a conscious choice to stop growing because of fear, doubt, difficulty or hardship. Sometimes we have unconsciously chosen to stop developing by not realizing that what we believe in is actually holding us back. We can become distracted, placing our efforts and attention elsewhere. We can also delude ourselves into believing that we are moving forward when really we are just spinning our wheels.

One of the most formidable barriers we can encounter is believing that we have reached our potential and already realized every possibility for ourselves. When we have such a belief, then our growth will come to a standstill. If we were everything we could be, and if we had done everything we could do, then there would be no reason for us to be here. We would be somewhere else in the Universe that would support who we are. If we were fully conscious of our Truth, that state of being would propel us to a whole new and very different level of reality, a level that would be beyond this dimension. There would be nothing more that we would need to understand or experience on earth, and our lives here would have served their purpose. Regardless of the state of our being–mental or physical health–being here in any way, shape, or form means that our life here is still fulfilling an important purpose. That purpose is not only for ourselves but extends outward to others and to the Universe itself. Life's very purpose is to fill us with knowledge of our Truth and the Truth of the Universe. Not only do we learn and grow through our own experiences, but we also learn and grow through the experiences of others. Our role in the big picture is much larger and more far-reaching than we imagine. We are each shaping and growing our own consciousness and we are each shaping and growing the collective consciousness. Our role here is significant and our effort towards growth and realizing our individual potential is a very important endeavor for each of us, as well as for the Universe as a whole.

We are our choices and we create our reality from them. On some level, then, if our development has stalled, we have made a choice to stay in a place that supports our not moving forward. The

Universe is not keeping us in one place—we are. It is just as willing to create a completely new reality for us if we are willing to choose one. However, if our beliefs do not change and develop in a way that supports our growth, we will continue to be stuck and will be unable to move towards the realization of our potential. As hard as we might struggle and fight in an effort to break free, we will be held captive. Even though we may have chosen growth, our progress towards growth in consciousness will be blocked because there is something in our way.

When we reach a barrier in life, we have three choices: (1) we could stop where we are, (2) we could turn back, or (3) we could find a way to press on. As individuals and as a group, we have often used all three strategies. Collectively there have been times in our history when we have stopped growing in consciousness. There have been periods when we have actually even retreated, giving up the gains we had achieved in our progress. Human nature is a remarkable thing and we have had a history in the development of consciousness that has included progression, stagnation and even regression.

The Universe is revealing to us what we believe.

Where are we now? Are we moving forward or are we at an impasse? If we look carefully and honestly at our lives, we are going to see areas that need our attention. Our lives and our world are full of many challenging and difficult situations. As we will see, the challenging and difficult situations in our lives give us an opportunity to grow, but are we growing or are we stuck? If we look around, read, watch and listen, we can see there are many barriers and obstacles that continue to plague us. We are sharing this experience on earth together, in order to have the opportunity to learn and grow from each other. What are we teaching and learning from each other?

In our past and in our present there have been and there are people who have shown us powerful ways to push past our barriers. These people bring our attention to a need for change in what we believe about each other, our world, and ourselves. Many of the problems that we see as obstacles are not from a lack of resources or wherewithal, but from barriers within our consciousness. If we can open ourselves up to a change in consciousness, then the possibility and potential of what we can create—individually and collectively—will be beyond the barriers and obstacles that we are encountering. So many of us are not aware or do not believe that things could be different, that we could be different. We have not consciously grasped the far-reaching impact of what we hold to be the Truth. This is what has enslaved us for so long. We do not believe we can actually create the fullness of life we have dreamed of because we believe it is just a dream. We have separated ourselves from our potential. The real barrier is our lack of understanding of the power that is held in our consciousness. When we do not believe that something is possible, we then block our dreams from being realized in a powerful way. "Our problems" are not barriers or obstacles, they are just situations calling for solutions. Those solutions can only come about when we believe that they exist.

In many ways, we have accepted a structure of beliefs and rules that has become part of our cultural mindset; a structure built largely on external power, external truth and in turn bound by external limitation. We hold these things to be the Truth. While the alternative reality—the one that we say we would prefer, the one so full of promise—we believe is unrealistic and just fantasy. We have struggled in the external world and fought many of the same obstacles time and time again trying to find "that place of true promise."

The only place we can ever make a crossing into a new reality is on a bridge built in our consciousness.

We can make a breakthrough in consciousness.

For each of us who are willing to choose, there is a tremendous opportunity for growth right now in our own lives. To do so, we will first have to make a breakthrough, not in the barriers of this physical world that we see as being the most real, but in the real barriers of our consciousness. We will need to break down the faulty beliefs in our consciousness and rebuild a new set of beliefs in order to move into a new reality because the new reality that is waiting for us will require a new state of consciousness.

Imagine an explorer that chose to take a path into uncharted territory. Although such a journey can be exciting, it can also be quite difficult. To help insure their success, most explorers make an effort to understand what they are getting into, but many underestimate the reality of their journey. Even with the most careful planning and diligent preparation, they often encounter new, difficult and very challenging obstacles. They find themselves in situations that they had not planned for, anticipated or ever imagined would happen. Many explorers are not successful because they stopped, turned back or lost their way. However, some explorers are successful and find what they were looking for and, in some cases so much more. What is the key to their success? Is it their preparation, their strength, their endurance or their determination? All these attributes are certainly very important, but there is something more–a special kind of ability. It is not just being able to utilize effectively and efficiently what they have. It is more than having knowledge or possessing skills, because the knowledge and skills the explorers carry with them are often unsuited for the new reality. We might say that their success is due to their intelligence, creativity or cleverness. All of these characteristics are certainly part their success, but to really define what allows them to be successful would be to say that it is their open–mindedness. They are able to see things in new ways and to radically change and revise their consciousness to "fit" a new reality. There is flexibility in how they approached the situations that they face. Successful explorers are able to see things from a new perspective, unconstrained by the past. They free their minds to be open to a new reality and to a new understanding–to a new state of consciousness.

This journey into a new state of consciousness will require the same kind of ability from us. For us to move forward into a fuller expression of our Truth, we will have to open our consciousness completely and freely to the process of transformation.

Openness is the pathway to our greater Truth.

To make a breakthrough into a new state of consciousness we will have to make a choice–to be open. If we do not open ourselves up to new possibilities and potential, how will they find their way into our lives and into our reality? For us to step into a higher level of understanding and push past the barriers in our consciousness, we will need to step into a new way of being called openness. Openness is the pathway that we can take to greater understanding of who we are. Each one of our lives is our own personal journey towards discovering the Truth of ourselves and of the Universe. When we consciously choose to open the doors in our consciousness, we are engaging a very powerful process in our lives. There is amazing potential and possibility waiting to come into our lives and into our reality. We have kept a large portion of what the Universe holds for us at bay, because we are unaware that it is just waiting for our permission to manifest in our reality. Openness is giving the Universe permission to come into our lives fully and abundantly. It is a way of being that can unlock the tremendous power and potential of the Universe to transform our reality and us. Openness is actively engaging the power of our consciousness to expand and develop into its full potential. In order for us to grow and expand into our potential, we have to make a far-reaching choice: to change. Growth is changing that which we hold within our consciousness. When we change what we know about ourselves or about our world, we are stepping into a new level of understanding. Therefore, growth is making changes in the very structure of our conscious reality. Openness is the willingness, acceptance and allowance of the Universe's powerful force of change to permeate all the areas of our consciousness and our lives. Openness is a process of restructuring our beliefs in such a way that they will support a new reality. Openness is a multi-faceted and multi-dimensional way of being that will require our full involvement. Openness is a new and conscious way of being that will take us where we want to go, to a place that we have chosen. Openness is the pathway to our greater Truth.

If we choose to pursue a greater understanding of our Truth, our choice will not be lost in the magnitude of the Universe and we will not be all on our own. When we make a conscious choice to grow, to open ourselves up to an expanded understanding, we may not realize the forces that we call into action. Yes, our choices in what we believe engage the Universe's power and potential in supporting our reality and present beliefs. Yet, something more powerful also happens. By choosing to grow and step into a new part of ourselves, we engage the Universe's power to support what we "can" believe in tomorrow—our greater consciousness. When we make the choice to grow in consciousness, the Universe will honor our request by undertaking a course of action that will provide us with valuable and rich opportunities for that growth. The Universe will do all it can to support us in moving into a new and more expanded reality. It will not be a reality that includes more of the same, but a new one, one that we asked for by making the powerful choice to grow in consciousness. If we were to be placed into a reality that was more of the same, where would the growth be that we had chosen? When we make the choice to grow in consciousness, the Universe will, in turn, unleash its power and call on its resources in an effort to reveal our Truth to us. The Universe will actively engage itself in our lives. It will endeavor to reach us in a way that will allow us to become conscious of the barriers that are holding us back, so that we may step through them into a greater and more expanded understanding of who we are.

We discover greater Truth by our openness to participation.

Not only is the Universe supporting what we believe in now, it is also supporting our growth into a new and more expanded understanding of who we can be. To support our choice to grow, the Universe has to move us from point A to point B in consciousness. The Universe has to do this very carefully without stepping on something quite sacred–our free will. On this path that we have chosen, we will encounter obstacles in consciousness, beliefs that are barring us from our growth and progress. For us to move forward, these barriers in consciousness will have to be recognized. Then we will have the opportunity and choice to change what we believe so that we may move to the next step in our growth. The Universe is not going to do this for us; this is something that we have to do for ourselves. The Universe could use all its strength and power to force us into making a choice that appears to have no alternative, but what would that accomplish? A choice made by a will broken under pressure, rather than a choice made by free will, is no choice at all. How strong can that choice really be, if it is one that was not chosen freely? If that choice requires us to do something from strength, how much of our heart is going to be in our effort?

When we have made a choice fully on our own, we are able to put ourselves behind it one hundred percent. A half-hearted endeavor is rarely a success. It has no wind behind its sails to carry it to its destiny. To force us to make a particular choice is not valuing us as individuals. It is not building something from strength, but from ill will. If the Universe changed our mind for us, where does that leave us but on the sidelines? What we believe in is our choice. We are in control of our destiny. It is our responsibility to make our own choices, and it is all of our choices combined that creates the reality that we share with each other. These collective choices come from what we believe individually. When we are open to participating with the Universe in transforming our own consciousness, we are not just moving towards a greater understanding of our own Truth. We are also moving towards a greater collective Truth that the entire world shares.

The Universe is ready and waiting to support our growth. However, it respects our choices and will only match our level of participation and follow our lead. If we choose not to participate in our growth, then the Universe must honor our choice and wait until we are ready and willing to venture forth.

*We discover greater Truth by our openness
to a new perspective.*

Choosing to be open allows for a new way of perceiving our reality—to see our lives and the world we live in from a new vantage point. This new perception will allow us to comprehend the Universe's support and guidance in our lives and to use that support productively. We have struggled and fought against many barriers in our reality because we have not understood their purposes and roles in our lives. The unexpected, challenging, and mysterious situations that come into our lives are serving an important purpose. These events are the Universe asking us, if we choose, to gain a new perspective, to gain a new understanding, and to gain a new level of consciousness. Powerful experiences can be powerful opportunities for growth. We can perceive these experiences in life as hardships, things in our way that hold us back and make life difficult and tiresome, or we can perceive them from a new and higher perspective–a new state of consciousness.

A step towards breaking through the barriers in our lives is to see them in a new way. We must become aware of and recognize them as having specific and personal reasons to be in our lives. The reason we cannot see why we are not moving forward and what is stopping us is that we are not looking at these challenging situations from this higher perspective. What we see as barriers are there specifically for a purpose. They are there to show us something that needs addressing for our growth and progress to continue. Taking this position gives us a completely new and greater vantage point from which to view our lives and their directions. If we choose to take this perspective, we are stepping into a powerful new state of consciousness.

We discover our greater Truth by our openness to recognition.

Our journey through life is full of all kinds of experiences, rich opportunities for growth and development. Opening ourselves up to seeing our lives and our reality in this new way can allow us to grow quite dramatically. We must be open to recognizing that everything in our lives is serving a purpose in some way.

One of the most important steps in using the opportunities in our lives is being able to recognize them. Openness to recognition is being open to seeing the deeper and greater Truth of a situation. We can become blinded by what we believe about the world and can become caught up in its many illusions. Growth in consciousness will require us to look beyond our illusions, the ones created by us and the ones created by others.

The illusions in our lives and in our world come from our inability to recognize the greater Truth of something. When we are not open to greater understanding, then we are bound by our assumptions. To break free of the barriers in our lives requires a willingness to challenge our assumptions and a willingness to open ourselves up to seeing in new ways and to considering new possibilities.

There are many signposts in life that we miss, ignore or pass right by. For example, a person who drives over the speed limit might get pulled over and receive a hefty ticket. When the police stops them, they have the opportunity to gain awareness about behavior that is dangerous and irresponsible. They may choose to make use of the experience to grow in consciousness, or they may not. The cost of the ticket may help bring to their awareness that speeding is not a good idea or they may choose to continue to drive too fast, disregarding a clear and direct message.

Being open to recognition is looking deeper into our experiences in an effort to gain greater consciousness about ourselves. If the police stopped us what would we believe about the experience? We might believe that we have everything under control or we might believe that the rules apply to others but not to ourselves. We might believe that the police have nothing better to do than to set up "speed traps."

If we continue to hold on to the same beliefs, we will continue to drive over the speed limit. We may receive ticket after ticket and, if we do not change what we believe and get the message, we may loose the privilege to drive or we may cause an "accident" that may have severe consequences both to ourselves and to others. Continuing to drive carelessly in spite of clear and sometimes numerous messages from the Universe saying, "Hey this is not a good idea!" is not being open to recognizing the opportunities in our lives to grow in consciousness. The Universe is actively engaged in each of our lives, supporting our growth in consciousness. Yet, we can fail to recognize clear and direct communication from the Universe about our beliefs that we may think are moving us forward, when actually they are holding us back.

We discover our greater Truth by our openness to listening.

We often go through life disregarding our experiences and not listening to what they have to tell us. This may seem obvious to some, but many times our growth is blocked simply because we dismiss, ignore, and fail to listen to aspects of our lives that are speaking directly to us. The Universe is always speaking to us, telling volumes about ourselves. The person who speeds is not just breaking a traffic law; they are breaking a law of a higher order.

The warnings that they are receiving are not just from the police but also from the Universe. Someone who engages in dangerous behavior is not in touch with the responsibility they hold for their choices. They are not conscious of the power and potential that their choice to drive over the speed limit can have in their life and the lives of others. A reckless belief system will create a reckless reality. The Universe is speaking to them very directly, making a real effort to reveal their unconsciousness.

Listening is vital for growth in consciousness. Being open to listening is making the powerful choice to be receptive. Receptivity is a willingness to receive the support and guidance of the Universe. It is being open to receiving information from all the many ways that the Universe can speak to us. We can disregard very important communication because we are not open to accepting it from some sources. We can fail to hear these messages because they can come from people, experiences, and things that we may believe are not valid, credible or applicable to us. We can find ourselves paying close attention to someone in authority and then coming home and disregard our child's insight and candor. Growth and development requires enrichment; when we are open to listening, then we actively are supplying our consciousness with many sources of sustenance.

To grow and develop we must learn to listen to the Universe and value the communication we are receiving. Opening ourselves up to listening is going deeper that just hearing, it is also listening in other ways. Openness is multidimensional and therefore we must listen with more than our ears but with something that can be even more receptive—our heart. There can be barriers and obstacles in our lives that just do not make sense and as hard as we may try to figure them out we can find ourselves at a standstill. Listening with our heart can often help us break through the barriers in our lives. There are times when reasoning and logic can fail us and we must find our course in another way. When we are willing to let our heart guide us in times of uncertainty and confusion, we are opening ourselves up to listening in a very powerful way. Some of the most profound breakthroughs in understanding can occur when we approach a barrier or obstacle with an open heart. When we choose to open our entire consciousness up to listening, we access a greater level of knowledge and wisdom within us and within the Universe.

We are multi-dimensional beings and are able to hear and discern in ways that can transcend our intellect. When we are willing to trust, value, and listen to our feelings we can make great strides in growth and discovery. Trusting what our heart has to tell us can often go against our reasoning and our logic. There can be decisive and pivotal points in our lives when we have to choose which aspect of ourselves we are willing to listen to the most. Does our reasoning have the final say or do we listen to the authority of our heart? Where we place our trust has powerful implications and can result in very different outcomes. We have often separated our intellect from our feelings as if they were two worlds distinctly different because we experience them differently. Our consciousness is not solely a dimension of the mind, but is a multidimensional energetic portion of the Universe. Not all the energetic potential and possibility of the Universe is able to come through just one sensory system. For us to access the fullest and most expansive Truth we can; we must be open to receiving information in multiple ways.

There are times when we have a sense of something, a "gut" sense, that is strong and at the same time quite elusive of our reasoning and understanding. These very intense sensations are not random or extraneous phenomenon but a response to an energetic reality on some level; it is another way of being conscious. These powerful experiences are the Universe's efforts to get our attention and gain our consciousness about something. We have often disregarded these phenomenon as unreal because we often do not understand these sensations and yet we experience them frequently. To be open to what the Universe is telling us, we must acknowledge the reality of our all our experiences, the external and internal ones. All that we experience in our consciousness is a result of an energetic interaction that has a reality in some way and on some level. When we learn to acknowledge and trust these experiences as real, valid, and of importance, we discover a huge source of support and guidance in our lives.

When we choose to grow, we give permission for the Universe to help and guide us. Openness to listening is being receptive to all the many forms of support and guidance that the Universe can have in our lives.

> *We discover our greater Truth*
> *by our openness to questioning.*

It is much easier for us to change a belief we are conscious of and know the reality that it generates for us. The people, experiences, and things that we do not understand and that do not seem to fit in our lives, come from our unconscious beliefs. These beliefs are often ones we may have never evaluated as being important or powerful in our lives. When the unexpected, challenging, and mysterious show up in our lives, we need to be open to asking ourselves, "What belief do I have that would bring this into my reality?" To grow, we need to take an active role in questioning the reality of our consciousness and the reality of our physical experience. If we are not aware of what our beliefs are, we are not going to understand our lives. If we are not aware and paying close attention to what is in our lives, then we are not going to be conscious of what we believe. The two are inseparable from each other and each holds a key to the other. If we want to understand something in our life, we need to ask ourselves, "What do I believe about this aspect of my life?" If we want to understand what we believe, we need to examine and evaluate the people, experiences and things that are in our lives.

If we wait for the Universe to bring our attention to beliefs that may be out of alignment with our goals and blocking our progress, then we are not taking an active role in our lives; we are taking a passive one. On the other hand, if we are open to questioning, then we have also opened ourselves up to understanding. Questioning is the first step towards understanding. If we do not question something, then how can we expect to understand it? Questioning is a request for understanding. The Universe is structured to support us and respond to our requests in all forms. We submit requests to the Universe in many ways. As discussed in the Second Law of Truth, every belief we have is a request to the Universe to support the reality of that belief. A question is no different; it is a specific request that has an energetic structure that draws a response to it. We have chosen growth and the Universe is supporting that choice, but we cannot get there without understanding. When we question, we are actively reaching for the golden ring that we have sought for so long. We are reaching for greater understanding and higher consciousness. We are reaching for Truth. We have opened up a large doorway and have engaged a tremendous driving force in our lives: asking the Universe to help us grow in consciousness. Within that seemingly simple request are powerful and far-reaching questions. Who am I? What is the Universe? What can we create together?

However, the Universe will not answer us unless we first ask; remember free will. The Universe will not give us something that we have not asked for. When we ask a question, that question sets up an energetic equation that compels the energetic structure of the Universe to find a solution. That solution can then flow into our reality. It may flow into our conscious reality or it may flow into our physical reality. It all depends on how open we are to receiving communication from the Universe and understanding its message.

There can be very challenging and painful experiences in our lives and the lives of those around us, like injury, illness, or death. These events often make us ask some very tough questions. We may never have asked these questions if those situations had not presented themselves in our reality. Those experiences can draw out and clarify some very important and unanswered questions that we may be holding within us. These are questions that we may have placed aside, forgotten, or decided were of no importance. If we do not actively seek understanding through questioning, then we are relying entirely on the Universe to carry us towards understanding. Part of our journey is to pick our own path and when we ask questions, we are leading ourselves towards our own conscious understanding. If we go through life and never question, how will we ever grow?

When we question death, we can learn about life. When we question loss, we can learn about what we have. When we question what the Universe is, we can learn about ourselves. For us to grow and move into a greater level of consciousness, we have to choose to be open to questioning.

We discover our greater Truth
by our openness to understanding.

Once we have opened ourselves up to growth in consciousness, we then have invited understanding to flow into our lives. Choosing to be open to understanding is choosing to place our trust in a very powerful belief: answers can be found. The Universe is a large and immense place of endless potential and infinite possibility, but all that it contains is not outside of us or beyond us. The Universe is us. We are part of the Universe and, therefore, we hold within us the answers to all the questions that we could ever ask. Being open to understanding is being open to the possibility and potential of the Universe. We create limitations and barriers in our lives when we do not believe that there are answers to our questions or solutions to our problems. Such a belief is telling the Universe to support our ignorance rather than to support our growth in consciousness.

Being open to understanding requires our whole involvement. Openness requires our whole being by seeing, asking and listening in new ways. The more we open ourselves up in as many ways as possible, the more we are able to tap into what we already have within us–the answers to our questions. Those who are open to understanding are open to all possibility and all potential. The potential of the Universe includes <u>all</u> potential, and some of that potential is in our reality right now. Sometimes a breakthrough in understanding comes about by recognizing that something we already have within us is the answer; It just was never considered as being a possibility. Frequently, we are looking outside ourselves and outside of our present reality in an effort to find something that will solve our problems and answer our questions. To be open to understanding, we must embrace a great Truth: the Universe is complete and so are we.

This Truth is telling us that the answers to our questions are already at hand. In fact, they can be right under our noses. The people, experiences, and things that are in our lives right now hold a very important purpose for us–they are supporting our growth towards understanding. Within our reality and within our very being right now is untapped potential. There is potential that is simply waiting to be unlocked in the people, experiences, and things around us.

For example, a job that is demanding more and more time from us may be the Universe asking us to gain a new understanding about what we believe about work. If our child is angry and frustrated by our absence from home, the Universe may be asking us to reach a new understanding about what we believe about our family. Our lives are rich with potential to grow in understanding about who we are, what we value, and where we are headed.

The moment we are able to understand the people, experiences, and things that are in our lives right now and what they have to tell us about what we believe, then their purpose is served and they can be released to become something else. The barriers in our lives are often the result of our misunderstanding the people, experiences, and things that are in our present reality. We cannot move into the future until we are able to resolve the present. When we are able to reach an understanding in our lives, we change who we are. We become something different by stepping into a new level of conscious understanding. That new understanding requires our reality to change so that it can support who we have become. If something in our lives remains or continues to reoccur even after we believe we have comprehended its message, then it is still serving a purpose for us in some way. The Universe will not keep doing something that does not serve us or support our belief system. If we make use of something's purpose, then its role is fulfilled and its job is completed. However, if we do not understand something in our lives and the role that it is playing, then it will continue to remain with us until we do. The Universe will continue to work towards raising our awareness and gaining our attention about something that needs addressing. The Universe will use its power and creativity to get our attention. If it cannot reach us in one way, it will take another approach. There may be changes in the people, experiences and things in our lives because of the Universe's efforts to get our attention and gain our understanding. The Universe will not give up on us because it is committed to supporting us one hundred percent. It will do everything in its power to get our attention about something that is standing in our way of realizing the potential of the choices we have made.

We discover our greater Truth by our openness to adversity.

Through our journey in life, we will find ourselves struggling, challenged and frustrated from time to time. Such situations say something very important—we are not lost or off course. Adversity is not the Universe trying to block our progress or steer us in another direction. Adversity is a pathway to growth. We may feel like we are struggling to find our way in life. There is, however, something working much harder to find its way to us. It belongs to us. It is our greater Truth. Whatever we are encountering in life that is difficult, the things that are challenging us are not random or extraneous occurrences. It is the Universe, itself, reaching out to guide us towards greater consciousness of who we are.

When we look at our achievements, individually and collectively, the ones that have the most meaning and value to us are the ones that we gained by our effort and determination. Most accomplishments, the ones that have brought us tremendous amounts of growth and great discovery, were often extremely challenging and difficult. We all wonder why life is so difficult at times. It is because through those difficulties and hardships, we learn and gain the greatest understanding of ourselves. We need to be open to adversity in our lives— not a force that holds us back, but rather one that can drive us forward into a new and deeper understanding of our Truth.

The natural world is the beautiful creation that it is because of the interaction of two powerful forces—life and adversity. When life struggles, it develops. Life has fought endless battles from the very beginning, seeking to find a way to exist in a world that is constantly challenging it in so many ways. If life never faced adversity, our world would be a wholly different place. In fact, without adversity the existence of life may not even be possible. Balancing forces created by different competing forms of life and the resources they rely on creates a co-existence or equilibrium to be established and maintained. If one form of life was able to multiply without restraint, then things would get out of hand rather quickly. Many times, in nature, this does happen and populations soar in numbers and then crash because they have exhausted their resources. It may seem that adversity would limit life, but actually quite the opposite has occurred. Nature has learned to use the force of adversity in a beneficial way. It is in the course of overcoming challenges and obstacles that growth and development of life has happened, filling our world with an immense display of diversity and sheer creative genius.

In order for us to move forward in life, we need to be open to adversity, to be able to accept and even embrace difficulty and hardship. Within each of our own personal journeys in life, we can discover much about who we are when we struggle and even "fail." When we choose to be open to seeing all our experiences from a higher perspective, they can play a large and productive role in our growth. Seeing our lives and everything in them from this higher and more conscious perspective will transform adversity into a powerful and creative force in our lives.

Thomas Edison was a great inventor and was able to bring forth many important and valuable discoveries that dramatically changed the world we live in. One of the most famous of his inventions was the light bulb. Today we look at a light bulb and see something that appears to be so simple, and yet is invaluable to us. However, the pathway that led Thomas Edison to the light bulb was long and arduous. He worked tirelessly experimenting with numerous different light bulb designs in an effort to find the one that worked. Some might say that he experienced failure many times in an effort to find his way to success. However, Thomas Edison and other creative people like him understand the important role that "failure" plays in leading them to success. When we are open to adversity and even "failure," our experiences can then become very productive and play a pivotal and powerful role in guiding us to our own personal success.

The Universe does not create or act without purpose. The Universe does not "fail" and it does not see anyone or anything as being a "failure". Every outcome is purposeful, beneficial, and serves us in some important way. There are no losers in the Universe. The Universe does not create loss. Humankind makes the judgment that this or that has no value. What we have seen as "failure" has the potential of becoming something of tremendous value to us. If we can learn to be open to understanding failure's purpose and role in our lives, we can truly benefit and grow in consciousness.

We discover our greater Truth by
openness to the unexpected.

In life, we often experience the unexpected. When we are young, many of our experiences are unexpected because we are experiencing them for the first time. Our childhood is often remembered as being full of rich experiences because we did not limit them by expectation. As we grow and mature, we become more seasoned by life and we tend to predict, anticipate, and even expect things to be and go a certain way. It is only natural for us to use our knowledge and experience when we can, to facilitate our lives and help us make choices.

Those choices are often based on what we believe will happen or can happen if we follow a certain course in life. However, expectation can actually get in our way and in the way of the Universe. Expectations can limit the possibilities and potentialities of the Universe. When we have an expectation, which is a belief, that expectation can narrow the channels through which the Universe can bring to us what we say we desire. When we expect that things can only be or go a certain way, then we are actually telling the Universe how to work. Our expectations actually slow the process down. Expectation is literally telling the Universe "I want this and only this." We may end up waiting a long time, possibly forever, for just what we believe we want or need.

What we may expect is not always what is best for us. We often do not recognize that what the Universe is giving us or could give us would actually serve us better than what we expect. We need to trust that what we are getting from the Universe is perfect, because the Universe is perfect. If we ask for one thousand dollars and the Universe delivers one million, do we turn it down because it was not what we asked for? Having an expectation can work just like rejecting such a generous offer by the Universe. If we say we want just this and only this, then where does this leave the Universe? It narrows the possibilities. Beliefs are so powerful that we need to be very conscious of how we use that power; using it to set us free, rather than bind us up and hold us back. There is a very effective way of stating to the Universe what we want and desire and not limit the power and potential of the Universe by an expectation. We can clearly state to the Universe, "I believe I am, I can be or do or have this", and then add to the statement, "I believe that this or something that serves my greater good is possible." This is a very important addition to any belief because it allows the Universe to also bring us all the potential that can come into our reality that we may not even be aware is possible. We are directing our lives and still being open to allow the Universe to participate in powerful and often unexpected ways.

To grow consciously we must challenge our beliefs, push beyond our expectations, and grasp the true potential of both the Universe and ourselves. When we believe that we are only just so much and that we can only be this or we can only do that, we limit not only ourselves but the Universe's capability to act in our lives. The Universe will only support us to a level that we believe we are capable. The Universe will, however, work towards bringing us to the awareness that there is potential and possibility of being more. Yet, if we do not gain an understanding of that possibility, choose to believe in it for ourselves, and then trust in it, we will remain where we are. If we want to be more, we must use the tremendous power of our trust to reach for that higher level. We must believe that we can achieve it. There is no need to prove anything to the Universe. The Universe already knows what we can be, what we can do and what we can have. We are the ones that need convincing. We must believe that we can be more, that we have the capacity and ability to reach this greater, fuller and deeper level. We create the only barriers in our lives. The people who are the most successful in reaching their goals in life do not create barriers for themselves and they do not buy into the barriers that others believe in. They step forward and claim themselves, for themselves.

When we believe that we can only be, do, or have so much, then the Universe is bound by its obligation to honor our free will to make those choices for ourselves. The Universe can only support that which we believe we can be, do, and have. It is the belief in our limitations that makes us go only so far. We are the ones who build the barriers in our lives that keep us from realizing our full potential.

The Universe has already claimed us fully and completely, but it is waiting for us to do the same. The Universe is willing to support all that we are, if we are willing to claim that for ourselves.

We discover our greater Truth
by our openness to new pathways.

Expecting some specific thing to manifest in our lives limits the Universe and so can expecting that there is only a certain process or pathway. Our beliefs, in the form of expectations, can restrict and bind up our lives. If we think that the only way to get from point A to point C is to travel by way of point B, then that is an expectation. There are many ways to get where we want to go and to be what we want to be. For us to reach a greater level of consciousness, we must be open to the possibility that there may be other avenues and pathways for us to travel. We must be open to other ways for the Universe to deliver us the people, experiences, and things that we desire.

Our physical dimension has many rules and structures that make it work the way that it does. However, the Universe is immense, infinite and full of all potential and possibility. We need to be aware that we may not know all the structures, rules and pathways. It is quite possible that there is a shorter, quicker, and more efficient way to get from point A to point C. It may also be true that the Universe really knows that point C is not necessary and that we can go directly to point Y or even point Z.

When something unexpected happens in our lives, it is the Universe attempting to make a breakthrough to us, in an effort to bring our awareness to a new part of ourselves and raise us to a new level of conscious understanding. The unexpected is the Universe saying, "Get ready! We are going to work on your belief system." We were expecting the Universe to be a certain way and work a certain way. However, the Universe is full of surprises and is going to use them whenever it needs to get our attention. The unexpected can happen when there is a place in our belief system that needs restructuring. If we want to be something or bring something into our lives, but there is a weak spot in what we believe about ourselves or about our world, the Universe is going to show us that weak spot in order for us to grow. It is going to go right to that place of weakness so that we can become aware of it and strengthen it.

The Universe does not point out our weaknesses to diminish us. It points out our weaknesses so that we may be raised up to a new level of conscious understanding.

The Universe is bringing our attention to beliefs that need our focus and attention. These beliefs need changing in order for us to be what we want to be, do what we want to do, and go where we want to go.

If we wanted to run for political office, but we had a belief that we could not speak well, that weakness in our belief system will undermine our ability to realize our goal. That belief may come from actual experience or from our lack of confidence because we never had an opportunity to develop our ability. Whatever the source of the belief, the Universe is not going to let it go unnoticed. It is going to show us in as many ways as it can, what we believe about our speaking ability. We might get comments from those around us that we are not good at speaking. Someone may even tell us directly that we will never be elected to office because we are not a proficient speaker. We might give speeches that are strong in content but lacking in their delivery because of our lack of confidence in our ability. We may get message after message that says we are not good at speaking in public. What we are experiencing is not the Universe blocking our path. The Universe is not telling us that we cannot become a politician. It is simply telling us that we need to strengthen our speaking ability, so that we can become what we desire.

We discover our greater Truth
by our openness to choosing it.

Life is full of choices. Every experience, every person, and every thing is, if we choose, full of potential. As we now know, our choices are extremely important. However, it is not only what we choose to do, it is even more important what we choose to believe about the experiences that we have. Many difficult and challenging situations can be experienced in different ways. What we believe about the experiences that we are having changes how we experience them. The pain of bearing a child whom we want, have planned and prepared for, is different than the pain of bearing a child who is unwanted. A labor of love is quite a different experience from a labor of disdain. What we believe powerfully changes our experience of reality.

The Universe is not telling us what to believe about the reality that we experience. We have been placed in the incredible position of making that choice for ourselves. This is a tremendous breakthrough in conscious awareness when we can realize that we have been given the power and responsibility to choose our reality.

What we choose to believe about the purpose and role of our experiences in life will not only dramatically change our experience of them; it will also change the course and direction we will take in the Universe. The incredible power of what we embrace as Truth reaches beyond space and time and creates a real energetic pathway to the future. Choosing to believe that all of our experiences is the Universe supporting us unlocks a tremendous resource in our lives. We can utilize our experiences in a new way and use them like stepping stones that will lead us to greater understanding of who we are and what the Universe is, allowing us to grasp a larger hold on our Truth.

The Universe is not telling us what to believe. It is not choosing how we experience our lives–we are. We are the ones giving meaning to our experiences. Our lives and everything in them is the Universe giving us opportunities to make choices. We choose what we believe about everything in our reality.

We choose what we believe about who we are and what we believe about our purpose in life. We choose to believe what life is all about. Every belief is a choice that we make for ourselves. Every choice that we make has a set of possible experiences and outcomes that come with that choice. Within each of the possible experiences that we may have, we have the power to choose what they mean to us. When we make a final and definitive choice to believe what they mean, then that meaning takes root in our being. It creates our experience of reality. We can choose to live in a world that is empty, lacking and meaningless or we can choose one that is full, rich, and meaningful.

There is within us, a unique, individual, and personal reality of consciousness; that place where we experience life, is a world of our choosing.

Our greater Truth is waiting for us to choose it.

Whatever we decide our Truth is empowers that Truth to come into our reality. If we do not believe in something greater, how can we find our way to it and how can it find its way to us? We can only discover greater Truth by believing and trusting in its reality. When we believe in our ability to grow and to increase our knowledge and understanding, we open the door that allows us to step forward and meet that part of the Universe and that part ourselves.

The Laws of Truth are tools that can guide us on our journey towards greater understanding of who we are and all that is waiting to be brought forth through us. We are remarkable beings because of the boundless nature of our consciousness. Our individual power and our unique potential come from our ability to make choices. The most powerful choice we make is what we believe is the Truth.

Truth is a real force and a real power because it is the very essence of the Universe that we hold within our consciousness. Our Truth is our reality. The Truth that we hold within our consciousness is our sovereign claim of who we are and what the Universe is. What we believe to be our Truth grants the Universe the permission to make that our experience.

How much power are we willing to believe we have?

How much of what the Universe holds do we believe is within our reach?

What are we willing to believe we can create?

How we choose to use the infinite power and potential of Truth is up to each one of us.

Individually and collectively, we are our choices.

REFERENCE OF TRUTHS

I.
THE FIRST LAW OF TRUTH:
THERE IS AN INTERCONNECTION
BETWEEN EVERYTHING. 21

II.
THE SECOND LAW OF TRUTH:
OUR ENERGY IS REFLECTED BACK
TO US BY THE UNIVERSE. 65

III.
THE THIRD LAW OF TRUTH:
CHANGE ANYTHING AND WE CHANGE EVERYTHING. 81

IV.
FOURTH LAW OF TRUTH:
OUR HOME IS WHERE WE PLACE OUR TRUST. 105

V.
THE FIFTH LAW OF TRUTH:
THE UNIVERSE SUPPORTS OUR
TRUTH IN A PERFECT WAY. 119

VI.
DISCOVERING OUR GREATER TRUTH 147

www.ingramcontent.com/pod-product-compliance
Lightning Source LLC
LaVergne TN
LVHW011231080426
835509LV00005B/428